# A Priest's Journal

*The light shines in the darkness.*
*—John 1:5*

## Victor Lee Austin

# A Priest's Journal

A
*JourneyBook*
from
Church Publishing Incorporated  New York

"A Fragment of a Man " was originally published in *The Anglican* and "Care and Community"; reprinted by permission.
"Theologian and Parish Priest" is adapted from an article in *The Harvest*; reprinted by permission of SEAD (Scholarly Engagement with Anglican Doctrine).
"A Crazy Bird" was originally published in *The Living Church*; reprinted by permission.

Library of Congress Cataloging-in-Publication Data

Austin, Victor Lee.
        A priest's journal / by Victor Lee Austin.
                p. cm. - (JourneyBook)
        ISBN 089869356X (pbk.)
            1. Meditations. 2. Episcopal Church--New York. I. Title. II. Series.
BV4832.3 .A92 2001
242--dc21

                                                        2001047714


JourneyBook and colophon are registered trademarks of Church Publishing Incorporated.

Church Publishing Incorporated
445 Fifth Avenue
New York, NY 10016

www.churchpublishing.org

5 4 3 2 1

## Acknowledgements

Although writing is an act committed in private isolation, the turning out of a book is a collective enterprise. I am humbled by the realization of how many people helped bring these writings from my initial computer screen to your eyes. There is Barbara Crafton who first suggested me as an author of a book in the JourneyBook series. Then there is my editor, Joan Castagnone, who drew the book out of me with the patience of an accomplished midwife. There are my colleagues in SEAD, who discussed a number of chapter drafts. And there are the people of my parish, who have allowed me to come into their lives and witness what God has been about with them. For all this company of witnesses, I give thanks.

*To my parents*
*and*
*to the people of Resurrection*

THESE MEDITATIONS are a varied lot, as is the life of a parish priest. A priest enters the market and buys groceries and worries about traffic, just like his or her parishioners. But then a priest will bury or baptize those same parishioners, and be taken into the inner recesses of their hearts. I find that I live in a world peopled by the folks I know, but that those people not only have names like Glenn and Kay and Nan, but Abram and Joseph and old man Job. My daily life involves asking why a young man died and why an old man finally had a son and why I love brick-oven bread.

I don't think you need to know much about me, but my editor says you'll be interested. If she's wrong and you aren't, please just skip ahead to the first meditation. I am a priest in the Episcopal Church, the rector of the Church of the Resurrection in Hopewell Junction, New York. Our parish lies in the Hudson Valley, about an hour and a half from New York City. We are a "family high church" parish, which means we love children and we also love incense and ceremony. For an Episcopal parish, we are about average-sized (average attendance is 100). I married Susan Gavahan when I was twenty-two-and-a-half (half my life ago) and we have two children, Michael and Emily.

On the side, as it were, I do several things. I am the editor of *The Anglican*, the quarterly journal of the Anglican Society. I founded and continue to produce, occasionally, a newsletter called "Care and Community," dedicated to the consideration of abortion—not as a political matter, but as a theological and church question. Presently I am also an adjunct instructor in ethics at Marist College in Poughkeepsie.

· · · · · ·

I am a candidate for the doctoral degree in theology at Fordham University. These meditations are being written as I continue to struggle with my dissertation. Nonetheless I can see that there is a deep connection between what I am saying in the two works. My dissertation research has involved a close reading of the social encyclicals of John Paul II. What I have discovered is that the pope strongly emphasizes Christ's union with every human being. This union—which exists prior to any evangelical act, such as gospel proclamation or sacramental baptism—is the source, for the pope, of human dignity, including human rights that all governments should promote and protect. It also means, for the pope, that Christ is so identified with each human being that he does not assert his right to *stand over* peoples or nations.

The pope's christological social vision, as I am describing it in my dissertation, has, I now discover, permeated my own pastoral practice. The young man who dies alone: I see him falling to the earth wrapped in Jesus' arms. The anonymous clerk who struggles to work with a crippled hand: I see Christ's hand. The tears of the mother in grief and repentance: they fall from Christ's eyes.

Often in these meditations, as you will find, I have suppressed the names. That is because, although we have probably never met, you may find yourself in one of them (and I would not want to get your name wrong!). If it is true that Christ has united himself decisively with each human being, then it follows that he has united himself decisively with *you*. May your journey lead you to the profundities of that very personal fact.

. . . . . .

FOR SEVERAL MONTHS we saw the green banners hanging on the lampposts of our town, banners bearing the town seal and saying "A Great Place to Live." I remember not that long ago seeing banners in New York City that proclaimed "New York City: Capital of the World." And I imagine there are banners down in the District of Columbia that say, "Washington, D.C.: The Nation's Capital." Call us humble then. Capital of nothing, we're just "A Great Place to Live."

I'm glad that I don't live in the capital of anything, and I'm particularly glad not to live in a place that styles itself the capital of the world. But I wonder what it means to live in a place that calls itself "a great place to live." What makes some place a great place to live?

Many of the stories of the Bible suggest that though there are great places to live in this world, most of God's people don't get to live there. Most of God's people, most of the time, are living elsewhere and are told by God to pack up and get moving. The archetype is Abraham. *Now the LORD said to Abram, "Go from your country and your kindred and your father's house to the land that I will show you."* And Abram, who was born in the place called Ur of the Chaldees, who had already uprooted himself and moved— with father and wife and brother and nephew and servants and cattle and all kinds of other critters of God—several hundred miles to a desolate place which they named Haran, and had lived there many, many years, once again leaves kindred and home and moves to a land that God promises to show him.

· · · · · ·

If we are true to biblical faith, we will always remember that on this earth we are but pilgrims. There is another country where our true citizenship is lodged and this place we live in, however great it is, is only ours for a while. A great place to live is a place that helps us get on with learning how to live as citizens of that other place.

*The kingdom of God,* Jesus often said, *is as if*—and then he would give a picture of the kingdom. It was often an agricultural picture. The remarkable thing about agriculture is that so much can come from so little. Tiny seeds can produce barn-bursting crops. A great place to live is a place where the seeds of God's kingdom have been planted. Our town is not the kingdom, not paradise. But can one see here the seeds of the kingdom? Do you find in your town, wherever it is, honesty, faithfulness, community spiritedness, concern for one another? Is it an environment that nurtures truth, and beauty, and goodness? Are there places in your town where you can hear, beyond the noise of life, the still small voice of God?

Those are the seeds that we should cultivate, and perhaps plant a few ourselves, we pilgrims who know that our ultimate destiny lies in another country.

AT FIRST they were quite worried. Not about the finances, they could handle that. It was her age: about forty. And it was the circumstances of the conception. "We were really drunk," she said. "I mean thoroughly, thoroughly drunk." Two healthy children already. A father who worked eighty hours a week. They wondered if they had time; they wondered about the fairness of the burden that a (possibly) very needy, handicapped child would lay on his siblings.

They knew their priest edited a pro-life newsletter. Perhaps that weighed on their decision, perhaps it was simply the ethos of a Christian community that welcomed all children. For whatever complex of reasons, they chose not to abort.

Cautiously, with quiet worry and struggling faith, she started to tell her church friends that she was pregnant. The news brought joy and support and prayers. Then there were scary developments. Though her soul welcomed the stranger who came knocking in the guise of an unborn child, her body began to give signs of rejection. She began to bleed, but then stopped, and, for the moment, things seemed to be fine.

Then she did what she wishes she had never done.

The medical profession urges pregnant women of her age to undergo amniocentesis. Without really thinking through what they were doing, she and her husband went in for the test. He tells me that the professionals who were involved with the test did everything as they were supposed to do. But unfortunately, about one time in a hundred the test causes the fluid to escape from the amniotic sac. She was that one-in-a-hundred person.

· · · · · ·

Normally when this occurs, the fetus, having lost its life-nurturing world, dies at once. This, in what turned out to be an extremely rare event, did not happen in her case. The fetus—or, to use the word that came naturally to her, the child—was still alive. Possibly the tear in the sac had closed. Possibly the fluid would regenerate. Possibly the child, whom the test had shown to be healthy, would survive.

The doctors sent her home to wait.

It was a terrible week. Prayers, tears, food brought by friends, their two still-very-young children full of questions, needing care, not quite able to grasp what was going on. Laying-on-of-hands. Guilt admitted and owned. This child, so ambiguously received, now hung on the edge of life, desperately wanted. "Why didn't we want him from the first?" And the psychological minefield question: "Why did I have that test?"

And God came. It wasn't what her priest said, exactly, or what she thought, exactly, but a voice she received from beyond. God came and told her he forgave those sins, those and all other sins. A grieving heart is close to God's breast. God said that he knows how we move from ambiguity into faith. God forgave all past actions in the light of their love for their dying child.

At the end of the week, a doctor confirmed what, by then, she already had intuited. The child had died. Labor would be induced. Then they would try to get on with their life. But with this difference: they would have a new heart of compassion for delicate, mysterious life.

. . . . . .

# Ask

· · · · · ·

THE MAN HAD BEEN CRIPPLED for years. He lay on his bedroll near the pool where, when the water became disturbed, he might have been healed—if he had been able to get to the pool on time. Jesus, with his customary entourage, was passing by. The man cried out to Jesus for help. Jesus said to him: *Do you want to be healed?*

Does he want to be healed! What a bone-headed question. The man is crippled. His life has a diameter that could be measured in feet. Does he want to be healed! Might as well ask if the slave wants freedom, or if the light wants to shine. Who—we want to put the question—who *wouldn't* want to be healed?

But the answer is not always easy. In a strange way, an infirmity, a condition of dependency, can become comfortable. Although no one wants to become ill, once a person has been infirm for some time, once one has endured disability for years—one can come to identify one's being with one's illness. Instead of saying, "I'm a person who has AIDS," we start to think, "I am an AIDS-person." Instead of, "I am a person who can't walk," we think, "I am a cripple"—that our *core identity* is as a cripple. I have a disease, therefore I am.

Jesus calls to us from outside the comfort of our dependency and asks us if we want to be healed. To be healed means to take up our bedroll and walk. It means to walk away: to set up housekeeping, to become responsible for ourselves. We will have to join the common lot of Adam's descendants and work in order to live. And, even more, we will have to become responsible servants of Jesus and start to care for others, since none of us is a person unto ourselves.

· · · · · ·

To be healed means, in that aspect of our life where healing comes, that we cease being simply the recipients of kindness and we take on the grown-up, healed identity of grantors of kindness. Jesus' question could thus be rephrased: *Do you want to leave behind your dependency and become more fully a human being, with the responsibility and power to care for others as, heretofore, others have cared for you?*

And if you want that, you have to ask for it. Jesus makes the man who has been crippled ask, precisely, for his healing.

The story poses for each of us a very specific question. What, exactly, would we like to be healed of? Some of us have physical ailments for which, yes, we would like to have healing. Others of us may think of spiritual conditions (let's not be too quick to call them "sins"), aspects of our personality that are not altogether beneficial to others, and yet we are loathe to have them changed. It would mean, we might say, growing up.

For it is easy, the work of an instant, to proclaim that we regret the grudges we carry around with us. But if Jesus offered us healing from our grudge-bearing habits, we might well hesitate at the cost. There is a certain pleasure that one gets from carrying a grudge, just as one can enjoy picking at a scab. Keep picking, of course, and the wound will never heal (and the pleasure of picking will never go away).

Do you want to be healed? Funny, Jesus, that you should ask that question. . . .

DISAPPOINTMENT FOR A PRIEST is a danger ever lurking at the door. In traditions and congregations where preaching is highly valued, Sunday afternoon is the most treacherous part of the week. For no matter how "good" the morning's sermon was, no matter how many people may have felt touched or moved by the preacher's words, that is all over by the afternoon, and next Sunday's sermon begins to loom. It is a vicious trap so easily slid into, trying each week to out-do the achievements of the last, trying each week to best myself, in the absurdly impossible contest which, since I am running against myself, I am guaranteed to lose.

But the disappointment of failing to preach a better sermon than the last one every Sunday is but one of the disappointments lurking in the life of a priest. Another arrives in numbers: how many were in church this Sunday morning? If last week we had 138, but this week we couldn't even break 100, how come? I will start fretting. Where were the Simones today? And Alicia, is she unhappy with something I said to her? Charles, I fear, resents a vestry decision that didn't go his way. The Nicholses, once again, must have put school sports ahead of church. Why must marching band eat up so many Sunday mornings? On and on it goes. And whatever the attendance figure is, however good it might be this week, by Sunday afternoon it too, like the morning's sermon, becomes the mark to be surpassed next Sunday.

What's wrong with this picture? *There's no prayer here.* Once I overheard Bishop Roger White of Milwaukee talking about a study that showed a surprisingly high percentage of Episcopal priests—forty-five percent, I think he said—had stopped praying. For a large fraction of clergy, the only prayer was corporate prayer: the Eucharist and Morning Prayer, baptisms, weddings, and funerals. No private time, no solitary mulling over the Scriptures, nothing outside of church services. And I realized that it was true for me too: for long stretches of my ordained life, I was just too busy to pray.

But if a priest isn't praying, disappointment is ready at the door. No, not at the door . . . disappointment has already moved in and set up housekeeping, bringing his friends: self-pity, gloom, and bitterness. Yet these interior houseguests need not stay forever. If a priest goes to the prayer closet and lays his disappointment before God, God can do some house-cleaning. And God starts with a simple word: "I have not called you to be successful; I have called you to be faithful."

Suddenly the game is changed; there is a new measure. Not how many are here, not how much are we doing, not how dazzling and moving is my sermon, but *Am I being faithful?* Numbers can be a sign of faithfulness, but they are not infallible. A drop in attendance or stewardship or some other barometer of parish life, *could* mean that I am falling short of the faithfulness that God demands of me, and that perhaps I should look for advice and try to change what I am doing. But a drop in the parish barometer could just as well mean that in my faithfulness God is leading me, and my parish, into a time of wilderness.

I can't go to the prayer closet once and get everything solved. I have to keep going back. For the question of faithfulness is the question of trust. God wants to know, "Do you trust me?" Week after week—tedious week, high week, dry week—God asks, "Do you trust me?" And even though I have preached upwards of five hundred sermons, I must take the next sermon and say once again, I don't have to be successful, I only have to be faithful.

. . . . . .

A PRIEST'S EFFORTS to build up a parish are themselves bound to lead to disappointment, for they are part of the struggle to claim a secure footing in a world that will ever remain transitory. My parish has a cemetery, and some people—even some young people—still buy plots for their burial. But most people will move on within, I'd guess, five years or so. While our parish has its share of people who were born here and plan to die here, transition is the lot of most. And transition makes it hard to build up a parish.

For instance, take Kay. A young mother, she came to our craft fair one year and struck up some friendly conversation. A parishioner discovered that church was not part of her life, and asked her if she'd like to come back on Sunday. She did, and brought with her a son, a baby girl, and a husband. We connected well, and shortly they were persuaded that there was no better time for their daughter to be baptized than at the midnight Easter Vigil. (Yes!) Another year, and Kay and Gerald, her husband, joined the Episcopal Church. (Yes!) Another year, and Gerald was on the vestry, leading a capital fund drive for a new roof. (Yes!) Yet another year, and Gerald's employment had to change, and they moved to Connecticut. (Oops.)

They come. They go. For the parish, it was a loss: young life, young leadership, a period of development of gifts, obvious growth in faith—then a transfer away. Focusing on things like that, a priest can drop down into the dumps, and quickly.

Sundays come and go; parishioners come and go. But I find that these occasions for disappointment are also occasions for God to move into the priestly heart.

· · · · · ·

The question is in the focus. Take Gerald and Kay. They had come into our parish, and in it, came to a renewal of faith. They are now practicing Christians. Attitudes had changed in their lives. Their children were growing up with Christian instruction. Their going off to Connecticut was, God might say, an act of apostolic voyaging. For (as it turned out) they chose their new home, in part, because it was near a church; and in that church they have been active, giving some new life to a congregation considerably grayer than the one they left behind.

Everything in this life is characterized by its lack of a secure footing. Every church building is decaying (some, admittedly, faster than others). Fix the roof, and the plumbing needs updating. Fix the plumbing, then there's painting. Flooring. Insulation. Heating. Replastering. It never ends.

But to be a witness to the action of God in someone's life, to be, perhaps, even more than a mere witness, but a person who contributes his bit to God's work in someone's life, to see someone moved by providence, and then led on, still under providence: this is a source of joy. One enormous benefit of meditative prayer is that God can show us how to refocus occasions of disappointment into moments of awe. But it doesn't happen without prayer. Without prayer, I think of building up the parish, rather than co-operating with God. I think of sermons as "winners" or "losers," rather than as occasions of faithfulness.

But to see God's hand even in the events that disappoint—to see myself as having a role in something much larger than myself—to know that I am not the center of the universe, yet even so have a role to play in the cosmic drama of salvation: that is, in the true sense of the overused word, awesome.

. . . . . .

# Robert

. . . . .

I KNEW ROBERT first as the rector of a neighboring parish. He was famous for language that may, most charitably, be called colorful. I knew about his language because some of his parishioners had fled from it to the parish where I was then a curate. In time I came to know him as a man of generosity. Occasionally we would have lunch, and he often brought a book that he wanted to give me. One gift that I used daily for years was Howard Galley's *Prayer Book Office*. It contains the Prayer Book daily services, such as Morning and Evening Prayer, enriched, for example, with antiphons for the seasons and feasts of the church year. I discovered that Robert, appearances to the contrary, delighted both in bestowing gifts and in keeping high-church Anglican traditions.

Father Robert was ordained both deacon and priest before I was three years old. There is a lot of mystery in that much of life and there was probably much that must have needed the secrecy of the confessional. (I always assumed his habit of swearing was far from his only sin.) Father Robert was a committed catholic priest, one who truly believed in his very bones in the truths of the catholic faith—God has promised to act in the sacraments of the church, so when sins are pronounced forgiven in the sacrament of confession, they really are forgiven and no longer weigh against a person.

During his retirement, he supplied for my parish one summer while I was on vacation. When I was back we met for lunch. He said that he didn't want to be pushy, but he had liked Resurrection and he'd like to hang his hat with us and help out from time to time. He put his hand on my arm. "For free," he said; "I don't want any money." I

. . . . . .

flinched, thinking about his tendency to shocking language. But I liked him—and I particularly warmed to the idea of not being a lone cleric. So he came, and in a few short months my parish came to love him very much.

During that time he gave me his *American Missal*, a large book designed to be used on the altar, which contained an enriched version of the 1928 Prayer Book's Eucharistic rite with many additional ceremonies. It had been given to Robert early in his priesthood. The editors of this particular *Missal* were committed to beauty in the mass, dignity, and proper ceremonial so as to manifest the mass's true character as a sacrifice in which the offered bread and wine truly become the Body and Blood of Christ. Robert's *Missal* was well used. Yet in the middle of it he had pasted one of the trial liturgies that led to Rite II of the 1979 Prayer Book. Unlike some other catholic-minded priests, Robert was no mere traditionalist.

He lived the catholic truth that one can trust entirely in God's grace, particularly in the sacraments. For God has promised that he will assuredly dispense his grace through the sacraments. This gift of God occurs regardless of the holiness or worthiness of the priest. I could always sense that Bob believed this. Indeed, sometimes his gruff or profane manner seemed to say that he thought God's grace was especially manifest when the priest was unworthy.

His end came quickly. Just before the Christmas after he started helping out, he mentioned, oh so casually, that he was going to have some tests. The cancer, when found, was advanced. He had some chemo, but then they called it off. Yet even in his suffering he could be all courtesy. When I visited him during his final weeks, he unfailingly would ask me about my burdens, tell me a joke, and tell me he would pray.

Once some friends came and anointed him and prayed over him at length. He told

. . . . . .

me later that he was not at all used to that kind of prayer. "I've always been a put-down-your-money and get-the-sacrament kind of priest," he said, slapping the table as if he were laying down a couple of dollars.

I hope that in his illness he came to experience, through his dependence on God and others—particularly his wife—more of the subjective side of grace. I doubt he would be put off by the suggestion that he had some character developments to undertake in a place that might be called Purgatory. All of us do. But if, as you read this, there are agents of God working him over, he may well also be telling them a little joke, and asking them about their own struggles in life, and trying as best he can to put them at ease.

. . . . . .

# Job

. . . . . .

JOB WAS A RIGHTEOUS MAN, a good man who feared God and was honest with all his neighbors. Everyone knew about him and admired him for his integrity. And one day he lost it all. In quick succession four messengers came to Job. The first: "The oxen were plowing and the asses feeding beside them; and the Sabeans fell upon them and took them, and slew the servants with the edge of the sword; and I alone have escaped to tell you"; and the second: "The fire of God fell from heaven and burned up the sheep and the servants, and consumed them; and I alone have escaped to tell you"; and the third: "The Chaldeans made a raid upon the camels and took them and slew the servants, and I alone have escaped"; and the fourth: "Your sons and daughters were eating and drinking wine, and a great wind came and struck the four corners of the house, and it fell upon the young people, and they are dead; and I alone have escaped to tell you."

In one day, Job's whole world changed. Job's friends came to comfort him, but their "comfort" did not work, for they assumed that these evils came upon Job because of some sin he had done. Job argued with them, insisting that he had not sinned, that he had been righteous. Why then did these evil things happen to him, so many evil things one upon another in a single day? Against his friends urging that he must have sinned, Job insists upon his goodness, despite which, evil things happened to him. And Job sits it out with his friends for thirty-seven long chapters until, finally, "The LORD spoke to Job."

. . . . . .

Note those words: to Job. This is what Job has wanted—not an argument, not an answer; Job has wanted only to have God speak to him, to have the assurance that there is a god and that God cares to be with him.

To be sure, what God says does not seem that comforting. *Where were you when I made the universe? Where were you when the Big Bang went off? You think you know so much, tell me how thought occurs. Tell me how consciousness arises. Tell me how the bowels of the earth are channeled. You're so smart, tell me how a new day begins, how a man dies, where darkness and light are kept. Come on, Man, explain this to me.*

Yet imagine hearing God speak those words to you! Of course you would quake in your moccasins, you wouldn't be able to speak; but how awesome, how incredible, to hear God speak *to you*, to hear the thunder in his voice, to see the power of lightning bolts and not be destroyed. I imagine it would be like being in a small craft on an immense lake just after dark. The wind suddenly comes up strong, the temperature drops, you are cold in your T-shirt. It's pouring sheets of rain, rain blasting sideways, you give up trying to row, you fear capsizing, you fear drowning, you fear chilly death, a quick and too close blast of thunder, the sudden burst of the strobe-flash, the smell of lightning, and God says, "Peace! Be still!"

Or perhaps it would be like seeing a herd of pigs, at one moment peaceably snorting amongst the corn, suddenly take it in their mind to leap into the sea.

Or maybe it would be like seeing a man who had been crazy, violent, a man who refused to wear clothes, a man who had scars and gashes all over his body because he would run, rush, throw himself onto rocks and boulders, a man people had never been able to help—it would be like seeing that man sit peaceably with Jesus, clothed and sane.

. . . . . .

There is no "answer" to the problem of why bad things occur. But there is the assurance that God who made all things has in his power all the violent forces of nature and of human beings. Job heard God's voice, Job heard God speak to him, and it was the end of all desire.

# Nan

· · · · · ·

NAN TAUGHT SUNDAY SCHOOL for thirty years, teaching the preschoolers, whom she loved much. She died rather quickly. The first medical diagnosis of cancer was received during Holy Week, and before the end of the Easter season we were having her funeral.

I saw her just a few days before she died, bringing Communion to her hospital room. Communion, Christians believe, is the life of Jesus miraculously given for us as we journey here on earth. Think of it as rations for a journey, Old Testament manna, daily bread. When I arrived at the hospital a friend was there, with damp eyes. "She's sleeping," she said. I stood at the door of the room, and my eyes also began to tear. "I'm sure she'd want you to awaken her," she said, but I was far from sure that I wanted to disturb her. If she's only sleeping (I must have thought something along these lines), maybe this is only a dream, and she will wake up, and things will go back like they used to be. . . . A nurse arrived with a pill and settled matters. Nan sat on the edge of her bed, a small white pill in her palm. "I can't see it," she said. The nurse explained it was one little pill, and she told Nan what it was for. Nan took it, and with help, found the straw and had a sip of water.

I sat beside her. She looked hard at me, and announced, "It's Victor." I said, "I've brought you Communion. Would you like to receive?" She nodded, I took her hand, and we prayed. "Our Father, who art in heaven, . . ." Somewhere around "Give us this day our daily bread" her voice trailed off. I finished the prayer, opened the little silver box, and placed the wafer in her hand. "The Body of our Lord Jesus Christ." I then took

· · · · · ·

the other wafer I had brought, and consumed it myself. We shared a moment of silence. When I looked at Nan, she was still holding the host between her thumb and forefinger. And she said to me something that I will never forget: "I don't know what to do with this."

*I don't know what to do with this.* Whatever Nan's spirit meant by those words, whether they were merely words of confusion as her mental capacities were shutting down, or whether she had some spiritual insight given her in those waning hours as she held the sacramental Body of her Lord between thumb and forefinger, they are true, true words of profound honesty. I said them about Nan herself, only a few days later. *I don't know what to do with—this,* with this casket, this body no longer breathing, this hole in our life. Of course, in one sense, I do know what to do. I am a priest, so I will have calling hours, and a funeral, and say the prayers appointed, and receive again the Body and the Blood, and send *this* body off to its resting place. And life will go on. But what does one do with *this,* with the fact of death, with the human condition? *I don't know what to do with this whole human condition thing.*

When you realize you don't know what to make of your life, of human life and human death, then you are ready to hear the words of Jesus. *I have gone to prepare a place for you. In my Father's house are many mansions—resting places for travelers—and when I go and prepare one for you, I will come again and will take you to myself, that where I am you may be also.* Those words, from John chapter 14, I hear Jesus saying to Nan as she held him in her hand. *I will take you to myself, that where I am you may be also.*

Jesus has taken the entire human condition to himself. He lived our life from its microscopic beginning to its painful end. He had a friend, Lazarus, who died. When

· · · · · ·

Jesus was invited to come and see Lazarus's tomb, he wept. Later, after the nails, the spit, the spear, his own body was laid in a tomb, which was closed with a large stone, and in the darkness, Jesus' body cooled to room temperature.

From beginning to end, in sickness and in health, in cruelty and suffering, amongst greed, ignorance, and intrigue, and including death itself, *for our sake* Jesus has taken the human condition to himself. Although I don't know what to do with cancer and cold bodies, I do know that Jesus has made a decisive act of self-identification with every human being.

Nan held in her hands the one who holds her in his hands. She did not know what to do with the one who had united himself to her forever. "I don't know what to do with this," she said. I said, "You could eat it." May I say the same words to any of you who look upon a pall-covered body and feel the awful emptiness of not knowing what to do with this, may I say to you, "You could eat it"? Come and eat these travelers' rations, eat this food to pilgrims given.

I RECENTLY READ a little book entitled *The Diving Bell and the Butterfly*, by Jean-Dominique Bauby (New York: Alfred A. Knopf, 1997). It has nothing directly, yet everything indirectly, to say on euthanasia, physician-assisted suicide, and the beauty of even a most restricted human life.

The author begins with the view from his hospital bed as sunlight grows, and only gradually do we come to understand that he, the author, at forty-three, has suffered a massive stroke and now lives with "locked-in syndrome." All of his body is paralyzed, save for his left eyelid. And through that last bit of mobility this remarkable book came forth.

At night, he tells us, his alphabet letters dance for him. "Hand in hand, the letters cross the room, whirl around the bed, sweep past the window, wriggle across the wall, swoop to the door, and return to begin again. E S A R I N T U L O M D P C F BV H G J Q ZY X K W"(19). Just as the reader begins to doubt the author's sanity, he is told that these are the letters of the French alphabet arranged in order of frequency of use. They are arranged in that order, by the immobile man on the bed, for the sake of—us. You go to his room, and he will speak to you, answer your questions, and—if you are Claude Mendibil—dictate this book to you, slowly, letter by letter. You speak this alphabet, "E, S, A, R ..." until his left eyelid blinks, and then you have his next letter.

Who is Jean-Dominique Bauby? He was, as this book reveals, a literate man. On a Sunday without visitors to read to him, "I contemplate my books, piled up on the windowsill to constitute a small library. . . . Seneca, Zola, Chateaubriand, and Valéry Larbaud are right there, three feet away, just out of reach" (102). He was a father, at various times lover and husband, a man whose calamity was noticed in society, an important figure at the international fashion magazine *Elle*. He *was*. Occasionally he blinks out, "my magazine," only to correct himself. His former life is over. Now he is an observer, and more than that, both beneficiary and victim of the actions of the human heart. Some people lift him with indifference to his pain. A doctor sews his right eyelid shut without explaining the necessity of it, indeed without talking to him or noticing the frantic questioning that came from his left eye. (He was terrified that *both* would be sewn up, and his sole way to communicate cut off.) Yet others take special care to remember to close his door, or arrange his mail so he can read it, or simply to attend to his tiny means of conveying the thoughts and passions within.

Perhaps the saddest, sweetest paragraphs are these from the middle of the book:

Hunched in my wheelchair, I watch my children surreptitiously as their mother pushes me down the hospital corridor. While I have become something of a zombie father, Théophile and Céleste are very much flesh and blood, energetic and noisy. I will never tire of seeing them walk alongside me, just walking, their confident expressions masking the unease weighing on their small shoulders. As he walks, Théophile dabs with a Kleenex at the thread of saliva escaping my closed lips. His movements are tentative, at once tender and fearful, as if he were dealing with an animal of unpredictable reactions. As soon as we slow down, Céleste cradles my head in her bare arms, covers my forehead with noisy kisses, and says over and over, "You're my dad, you're my dad," as if in incantation.

. . . . .

Today is Father's Day. Until my stroke, we had felt no need to fit this made-up holiday into our emotional calendar. But today we spend the whole of the symbolic day together, affirming that even a rough sketch, a shadow, a tiny fragment of a dad is still a dad. (69–70)

All this from a man who has only a few square inches of feeling in his entire body, who cannot swallow even his own saliva, or hold his head in place, or do anything but dart his eye, slightly move his head, and blink.

Who is Jean-Dominique Bauby? A friend reports one answer, overheard in a restaurant:

The gossipers were as greedy as vultures who have just discovered a disemboweled antelope. "Did you know that Bauby is now a total vegetable?" said one. "Yes, I heard. A complete vegetable," came the reply. The word "vegetable" must have tasted sweet on the know-it-all's tongue, for it came up several times between mouthfuls of Welsh rarebit. The tone of voice left no doubt that henceforth I belonged on a vegetable stall and not to the human race. (82)

Is he a vegetable, a disposable rough sketch, a mere splinter of true humanity? No reader of this book could agree. On the contrary, one is continually struck by Bauby's polished quality, his honed emotional sensors, and the unshrunken dimensions of his mental geography. If you, this evening, as you drive to pick up your son to go to a play, suddenly feel yourself spinning, lose your focus, break out in sweat, and slip away . . . and sleep for nearly two months . . . and awake, paralyzed, would you say your life had

. . . . . .

lost all value? Would your friends say, before you awake, not knowing you can hear, "This coma has gone on too long, we should pull the plug and let him go"? *The Diving Bell and the Butterfly* is an argument to the contrary, an incarnational refutation of any dogma that would diminish the dignity of a human being.

THERE WAS SOMETHING I was going to write about today, but before I could get my computer altogether set, a common event occurred. The screen froze. I clicked here and there; typed, gingerly and cautiously, a key, pause, then another key, pause, then (abandoning caution) key upon key; clicked madly; nothing. Ctrl-Alt-Del told me that some program (whose name meant nothing to me) wasn't "responding"; I tried to delete it. For a minute, WordPerfect seemed, well, normal; then it twitched in such a way that I thought it prudent to close up the program and start again. It closed without delay, but stalled in the early stages of reopening. Click; key; even Ctrl-Alt-Del; nothing. I found a paper clip and pushed the recessed "reset" button.

When Windows 95 started to open, it realized the dastardly trick I had played upon it (so schoolmarmish: "Windows was not properly shut down" and we know who did it, don't we!). I was told to run ScanDisk. ScanDisk, today, decided to run on molasses. I went out and loaded the laundry. It was still checking files. I tried on a new shirt from L. L. Bean. It was still checking files. I went to the kitchen to refill my coffee. Now it was ready to remove some apparently useless bytes. "Take them away!" I said. Then it wanted to check the disk. I watched the yellow bar slowly grow across the bottom of my screen. Minutes passed. At forty-eight percent I thought of the percentage of the votes that George W. had received. At fifty-one percent I thought of WAMC's radio program on women. At sixty percent I realized I had finally seen a passing grade. I started converting the percentages to simple fractions: two-thirds, then three-fourths, four-fifths. . . . At ninety-one percent (ten-elevenths) I thought of the percentage of blacks that did not vote for George W. Finally ScanDisk was finished, and it released my computer to me.

Gone was whatever inspiration I had for writing; all I could think of was revenge. And the best revenge is humor. Did you hear about Bill Gates's toilet backing up? He phoned a plumber. The plumber explained how to fix the problem. "Close all your doors inside your house, go outside, close that door, lock it, wait 30 seconds, and then go back in; everything will be fine." Or the one about Dante's new circle of hell? It was created expressly for the person who wrote the dialogue box that reads, "This program has performed an illegal operation and will be shut down," and your one and only choice is to click "OK."

Some people say that technology is merely a tool, and that the moral issues with technology hang exclusively on how it is used. Such a statement is a truism that hides a more troubling reality. Modern technology aims to save our time and multiply the things we are able to do. Its very existence alters our reality: we are lured by its promises; we change our expectations; we place our hope in its story line of ever more, ever better.

Despite all appearances, I am grateful when my computer gets hung up. For although I'll grumble about the wasted time, fidget away the minutes, and make idle and senseless observations about its jargon and fix-it procedures, still in the midst of all that, my frustration mounting, I may actually hear that voice from outside. The voice that is the ultimate authority on illegal operations. The voice whose incarnate face is the true window into paradise. The voice who loves me much, much more than I love my gadgets.

. . . . . .

"CAN I COME BY this morning? I need to talk with you."

The woman's voice was urgent, so he named a time. She came and told her story. As he knew, she had two sons already of school age, and as her pastor he knew there were some stresses—financial and emotional—that she and her husband had to deal with. They couldn't imagine how to cope with the added burden of becoming parents of another child. "Awhile back we thought this pregnancy had ended on its own, and we were relieved. But now the doctor tells me there's nothing wrong—the fetus is just fine."

This was the first he heard of her pregnancy, and the first he heard of her plans to abort. She told him that the procedure was scheduled for later in the day.

He doesn't remember all that he said. She soon began to weep, and yet was determined to go through with it. She said her husband approved, that they had thought through all the options, that this would be for the best.

His first questions were of a practical sort, avoiding the moral dynamite at the center of their talk. "What if your boys ever find out? What if this is a very special daughter? What if a tragedy happens to your boys?" But they both knew these weren't key questions.

Then he began to weep. He says he begged her, literally begged her, not to abort her child. Her response was straightforward: "I knew you'd say that." Then why had she wanted to see him? In order to be told that she was planning to commit a dreadful sin?

It wasn't an effort on her part—then or thereafter—to change his mind about abortion. She wasn't trying to tell him that he was out of step with the times, or with other pastors. And she was, if this is possible, remorseful about what she had yet to do.

He also doesn't remember how their talk ended. ("I don't think we prayed. What would I have prayed for?") It was a dreadful afternoon for him, knowing that at any time, somewhere not too far away, one of his church members was going to have her unborn child "terminated." A death, freely chosen, and he had been unable to do anything about it.

It was a relief, in a way, that she didn't attend church the next Sunday, or the next. But then God, perhaps, put it in his mind that he should call her up. It wasn't easy. They agreed to meet for lunch. It began awkwardly. He tried to convey that his concern for her had not ceased. He shared with her that his wife had very irregular cycles and that, as a result, they often wondered if they were losing a child to an early, spontaneous miscarriage. He said this to convey that he knew something about the feeling of losing a child. With such indirection he tried to let her know that he didn't condemn her. She too talked of various things, letting him know that she wasn't rejecting him as her pastor, that she accepted his having pro-life convictions, which he in turn made clear were still very much his convictions. She offered to resign from her various duties at the church. He said that he didn't feel that was necessary.

It was a delicate lunch, but somehow at the end the dew of grace had fallen over the scene. They would go on as pastor and parishioner to each other. With his own eyes moist he heard her say, "I'm so glad you called me. I was afraid you'd never speak to me again."

. . . . . .

# The Survivor
. . . . . .

THE PROLIFIC AUSTRALIAN NOVELIST Thomas Keneally is famous as the author of *Schindler's List*, which showed us the ambiguity of moral good in the midst of evil. All of Keneally's novels take us to troubling psychic depths. I am haunted by a scene in his novel, *The Survivor* (New York: Viking, 1970), which literally wrenches painful truth out of the grave.

In the scene the corpse of an Antarctic explorer has just been rediscovered. The corpse was iced in its sleeping bag for forty years, ever since the expedition on which this leader had a serious stroke, deteriorated rapidly, and died. His fellow explorers left him where he lay. Now rediscovered, but under twenty-five or thirty feet of ice, the corpse is being pulled out by rope and pulley.

A man named Ramsey watches this scene. Ramsey was there when his leader fell victim to his stroke, and ever since he has carried with him an ignominious secret. Deep in his "belly" Ramsey has known, for these forty years, that when he left his leader behind, he was not yet dead. His belly has tormented him ever since, poisoning his thoughts and damaging his relationships. Nothing in his life has gone right or well. Now the resurrection of this corpse that was once his leader means a crisis for Ramsey, the kind of crisis that pits mind against gut.

Ramsey watches the resurrection. "The winch pulsed. From the ice it drew a burden strapped to a stretcher. When clear of the pit, the load began to spin crazily, four or five turns one way, three or four the other, and then lay still, though twisting in a slow arc" (265).

. . . . . .

There it is—a pitifully small bundle, swaying on the end of a hook. A speck on a sea of ice. This was not what he had expected. Or rather, this was only half of what he expected. His mind had foreseen precisely—and only—this "sad resurgence." But his belly had expected damnation.

He did something wrong forty years ago, and now it will be brought to light. He wants judgment and he fears it. In the event, there is no judgment, only the sad resurgence of the body long dead.

In our modern world many therapies help us to probe our past and understand our feelings and compulsions. These therapies are ropes and pulleys that bring to light things long hidden deep within. They perform an important function for many people. But the exposure of the past is only a "sad resurgence" if we are not able to pronounce a moral judgment on what has been brought forth. We need, in other words, not only therapy but also the concepts of sin and judgment, repentance and forgiveness. Without the possibility of judgment there can be no forgiveness. And without the experience of forgiveness there can be no hope for liberation from the past.

I have written earlier about the child who was a casualty of amniocentesis. It was crucial that the parents grieve and repent their ambiguous embrace of that child, in order for them to be able to move with freedom into their future. Ramsey, in Keneally's book, merely survives. He has not the capacity for repentance, and that is why, like so many of our contemporaries, he merely passes through his crisis—why his crisis does not heal.

. . . . . .

# The Face

· · · · · ·

I WAS ORDAINED A PRIEST just before Lent began, and just a few days before that a four-year-old boy of our parish had died. His death came at the end of a long illness. My rector, Michael Webber, was with the boy and his parents when death came. The child was connected to the usual monitors at the hospital. Michael watched the heart monitor's peaks and valleys gradually get further apart, and smaller, until there was just a straight line.

Preaching at my first mass, Michael used the contrast of the straight line, which on the monitor means death, and the peaks and valleys, which indicate a living heart, as a visual image of the season of Lent. On Ash Wednesday we confront the straight horizontal line: we are mortal, made of dust, and to dust shall we return. But having faced mortality, we can enter into Lent, a season of mountain climbing, like one heartbeat after another, until at Easter (or in Easter, at Ascension) we are able to see our Lord Jesus' "departure" (as St. Luke calls it): Jesus in his glory upon the mountain returning to his Father. Lent is an opportunity to play the usual story of our lives backwards, to move from dying to living, from the straight line to the mountain.

Just before Lent, the church takes us back up the mountain that Jesus climbed with three disciples before he himself confronted his own mortality and experienced the flatness of death. The event is named by the fact that, on the top of the mountain, Jesus' face was transformed into light. Transfiguration: the disciples beheld it, and somehow understood that whatever God touches turns into light because God himself dwells at

· · · · · ·

the heart of light. So the Transfiguration is their assurance that Jesus is truly the Son of God, an assurance that they can draw strength from when the bitter events culminating in the Cross come to pass.

Yet there is a mystery in the Transfiguration, a mystery that becomes clear when you realize that preachers tend to take two divergent lines of interpretation of this event. On the one hand, some preachers say that this story reveals something that is uniquely true about Jesus. Jesus is the Son of God, at the time of this story about to "depart," that is, die and be raised and return to his preexistent glory at God's right hand. When he is transfigured, his unique status is made clear to his disciples.

On the other hand, other preachers say that what is revealed in the Transfiguration is not Jesus' uniqueness but rather something that is true of every human being: that the glory of God lies hidden in true humanity. If we could see each other as we really are, then we would know that every human being we meet has been created by God who is light and thus every person *is*, essentially, light. Human being is one particular way that light exists in the world.

Is the Transfiguration a revelation of Jesus' uniqueness, or is it a revelation of true humanity? Another way to put the question is this: is the mountaintop event of the Transfiguration an unveiling or a veiling? When Jesus is transfigured, is his flesh as it were *pulled back* so that we can see who he truly is (and always has been) on the inside? Or is something added to him, is the light poured over him? The first choice, unveiling, corresponds with the event being uniquely about Jesus, and we are reminded of the phrase in Wesley's Christmas carol: "Veiled in flesh the Godhead see." The second choice, a further veiling, corresponds with what happened to Moses or to the burning

. . . . . .

bush where God seems to have poured himself over and around an already-existing natural reality.

I suppose that preachers have it both ways because both ways say something true. Jesus is unique, and yet he is the true Adam, the one who shows us what humanity really is. And when we are saved, God pours his light over us, like the waters of baptism, and yet this light is but the revelation of our original constitution as beings created by the word spoken out of the heart of light.

Shortly before he died, the mother of that four-year-old said to him, "It's okay, son, you can go home now." It is not likely that his human ears were capable of hearing those words. Not likely, yet not impossible. And I have a fancy that perhaps is also unlikely, and yet I suspect that you too may have had a similar fancy: that a person who has died is saying special prayers for you. I have fancied all these years that this child specially interceded for me on my ordination. He had gone home where the light was. "For now we see in a mirror dimly," St. Paul writes, "but then [we shall see] face to face."

IF YOU DO EVERYTHING called for in the Book of Common Prayer, it is the longest Sunday morning service of the year. For that reason, despite the questionable advantage of dividing a large crowd, at Resurrection we cancel the early service and have just one liturgy. In the undercroft the people gather, rather noisily, holding hymnbooks and programs and palm strips. The acolytes and I come down at 9:25 with thurible, torches, holy water; and, for this week only, a San Damiano cross, the image that Saint Francis was gazing upon when he sensed his vocation. You can hear the clatter of some percussion instruments that have been given to the children: tambourines, blocks, and triangles. Some people look nervously outside at the dark clouds. If it's raining, we'll stay inside and just process up the stairs. Otherwise, we go outside and walk around the church. In the final minutes I will tell them what Michael Ossorgin, my college tutor and a Russian priest, used to say: if it rains (or snows) on the Western Easter date, but the sun shines on Russian Easter, you can see which calendar God keeps.

The liturgy begins with some prayers and chants, which reverberate badly in this non-projective space. A lay reader or the deacon reads the account of Jesus entering Jerusalem: riding upon a donkey's back, cloaks thrown before him, and palm branches, and shouts going forth. Hosanna. Blessed is he who comes. Hosanna.

It is both serious and informal at the same time. A long chanted prayer, and then the asperges. The people lift their palms and I vigorously shake the aspergium, aiming holy water at all the people, even those in the very back. Many people smile; a few of the younger ones flinch.

· · · · · ·

Outside, we are a rag-tag band as we process around the church. The people up front are bravely moving ahead with the new refrain, "All glory, laud, and honor," at the same time as the people in the back are struggling to get to the end of the preceding stanza, "good and gracious King." Some percussionists are uninhibited, some are rhythmical, and some are shy. We stop before the front door of the church to give everyone the chance to get caught up.

I stand at the door and turn to look over the people as they close in together, singing yet another stanza. I see tambourines and branches and skiing caps and parkas. I see faces of dear ones I have cried with and faces that I haven't seen for many months. I see one face that comes only once a year: not for Christmas, not for Easter, but for today. And I see faces unknown to me: faces belonging to people in whose hearts, please God, something new is stirring.

It is a crowd, and it is exciting. Within the hour we will be kneeling in a chasm of silence, immediately after the proclamation of his death. Another half-hour or so, and in dimmed light, we will taste his final gift of body and blood. And another ten minutes, we will depart in silence unmarked by hymn or organ.

But at this point, at the door, on a chill morning of early spring, the faces are the proclamation of his triumph. Nearly 2000 years after the fact, the pageantry of Jesus' Entrance still has the power to draw a crowd. Something decisive has come to pass, something so decisive that even half the world away and eighty generations on, we still gather, still rejoice, still sing hosanna.

. . . . . .

"I CALL IT HELL WEEK," a Lutheran pastor once told me. It *is* a busy time. For during the Triduum (to give the period its old Latin name) a priest is almost continually employed in the re-living of the great events of our salvation. Yet after all the preparations, the weeks of Lenten discipline, the planning of the services, and the sheer expectation of it, I find that busyness of the Three Holy Days to be a sober yet ecstatic experience. From sundown on Thursday to the wee hours of Sunday one is taken out of oneself (the root meaning of ecstasy) and carried into a holy time. There is simply no time for anything else. Mail will pile unread; studies will have to wait; the commerce of everyday life, grocery store and bank and retail merchant—all this is put out of mind, for the mind is completely taken up with something vastly more important.

I like these three days because, once they start, it no longer matters whether I am prepared or not. My sermons are ready, or they aren't; the liturgical details are worked out, or they aren't. It no longer matters. The time for work is past: the time for the remembrance of Christ's work is upon us.

We celebrate Maundy Thursday in the evening. The church is bright with light. As you enter you see a few flowers, the first since Ash Wednesday, and in front, facing the pews, a dozen folding chairs in a semicircle. Our worship has a tender feel on this night, as if the gentleness with which our feet are bathed seeps out into everything we do. We have a procession, also the first since Ash Wednesday; we sing, we smile. It is the celebration of the institution of the Eucharist, and yet our gospel (if we read from John) contains no institution narrative ("Do this in remembrance of me"), but rather the account of the foot washing. At his final meal, the meal before the journey, our Lord took care to touch us with love. And with cosmic seriousness, he told us that there was nothing more important than for us to be gentle with one another.

It is a leisurely service. We like to sing the Ghanaian folk song, "Jesu, Jesu, fill us with your love, show us how to serve the neighbors we have in you." We sing it over and over. But then, as you know, the meal was over, almost abruptly. Jesus went out to pray, and the apostles followed; we consume, each of us, his Body and Blood, then carry the sacrament to a corner in the back of the church, where, surrounded by a few candles, he will pass the night in dim light.

Now the singing is ended. One or two persons remain with him, for now, while the lights dim and the people begin reciting the psalm that he recited from the Cross, *My God, my God, why have you forsaken me?* At the altar, all ornamentation is stripped and taken away. No candles, no color, no cloth remain. The sanctuary light is removed and the ambry door is left open, its contents gone. Finally all is bare and dark, save for the little lights at the back.

Through the night people will come and go to be with him in this singular spot, his home for this night of the year. Up front is bareness, a stark presaging of the day to come. But back here is the smell of beeswax and flowers, and the hope of a flickering light. If we were to give voice to our hope, we would probably say that we hope his prayer will be fulfilled. That we will learn to be gentle with one another.

. . . . .

# Joseph

YOU HAVE HEARD ABOUT his mother? A beautiful woman with lovely eyes, his father fell in love the moment he met her and was willing to work for seven years to obtain her hand in marriage. But there was deception: her father substituted her sister, Leah, and Jacob did not know—until it was too late. So his father had two wives. Leah was easily fertile; she had six children. His mother was barren, so in desperation she gave her maid to her husband, and her maid bore two children. Two children were also born to her sister's maid. Finally she gave birth, and her child is the hero of this story.

He was, of course, younger than all his half-brothers. Then his mother died while he was just a boy. He became his father's favorite, and his brothers became jealous. One day his brothers bound him and threw him into a deep pit, thinking to abandon him to starve, when a caravan came by. They sold him. His mother dead at an early age, himself not yet quite a man, he is sold as a slave and taken to Egypt.

He is one of *les miserables*, a small, miserable, unhappy creature on a vast, impersonal, unloving stage. What did he do to deserve his mother's death, his brothers' cruelty? What did he do to deserve being delivered into a world of slavery and hardship, buffeted by winds of world-events beyond his ken or control?

The answer is, nothing. He did nothing to deserve this. He could have died in the pit, abandoned; many have. He could have died on the road to Egypt, from disease or exhaustion, mistreatment; many have. He could have died in his cell in Egypt, forgotten by those few who once knew him, unknown by those many around him.

. . . . . .

This is the way the world is; cruel is the way the world is. And I wonder: what is the meaning of a human life in such a world?

The story of Joseph does not answer the question. But it invites us to have faith that God can work in hidden ways to give unexpected meaning to a life. For in the event Joseph does not die; rather, God prospers his hand. You know the story: Joseph finds favor with his captors, his owners, with those who have power over him. He comes to the attention of Pharoah who puts him in charge as his lieutenant over the entire land. And in that post, Joseph makes provisions for the famine foretold in the symbols of Pharoah's dream; he saves the world from starvation.

Including, at the end, his own brothers. Desperate, they travel to Egypt in the hope of food. There Joseph sees them, although they do not recognize him until he chooses to reveal himself. Then they are genuinely remorseful, but Joseph gives them heart. *You meant it for evil, but God meant it for good.*

It is hard to see the hand of God at work. Most miserable lives seem, in the end, just miserable. And even for those who die happily, as did Joseph's father Jacob, the years lost to deceit and discord cannot be given back. Yet we hear Jacob say, at the end, that if Joseph is alive, "It is enough." Actions for good, actions for evil—Jacob's life, Joseph's, his brothers'—there is ever hope that God is preparing in secret to resurrect unexpected meaning in human life.

· · · · · ·

WHEN I WAS A BOY, I used to wonder about the special names for the days of this week. The best I could make out of "Maundy Thursday" was that it was a mangling of "Monday," and I had not the slightest inkling that it meant *mandatum*, the commandment to love one another, ritually enacted in the foot washing. "Good Friday" posed a different problem. It seemed to me that the day of Jesus' death ought to be called Evil Friday.

It is good to puzzle through names, to have names that are puzzles, and I think our contemporary efforts to dumb all things down remove too much of the texture of life. I stubbornly persist, for instance, in reminding my Roman Catholic friends that the "real" Holy Thursday is Ascension Day, and that the Thursday in Holy Week is properly known as Maundy Thursday. But there is no disagreement on what to call this Friday. We call this Friday good. But why?

If you come at this day from, say, the familiar devotion of the Stations of the Cross, your emotions are fully engaged. This is what theologians call "Christology from below"; it is the way of Saint Francis. Your heart and eyes are turned to our Lord, who had committed no wrong, who would not have harmed even a bruised reed (as the prophet put it), hanging in agony, tormented in both body and spirit. His friends have abandoned him, and those who are with him spit, mock, and laugh. He may even think that his Father has abandoned him. Perhaps indeed he does lose his mind, perhaps the agony is so utterly extreme that he forgets who he is. Call this Doom Friday, if you must give it a name; but dare not look on that precious face and call this Good.

This, however, is not the perspective of Good Friday. On this day, guided by John's gospel, we take the Cross "from above." We look at the Cross and see a majestic victory. The apparent victim turns out to be the victor, a king whose physical weakness cannot hold back his true power. "Are you a king?" Pilate asked, and trembled at the answer; a mere glimpse of authentic kingship was enough to make this governor seek his release. John, who had reclined at his breast, best understood: this is a king who is ruling the world from his throne on the Cross. To Pilate: *You would have no power over me unless it had been given you from above.* To his mother and John, creating community: *Woman, behold, your son!* and *Behold, your mother!* To everyone: *It is finished.* These are not the words of a victim, but of a supremely confident authority, ruling, judging, providing what is needed for the future. And at the end he hands over his own life, which no one could take from him. The church always reads John's gospel on this Friday. It is with John's eyes that we call this Friday good.

It is the first perspective, the perspective "from below," that shows us the suffering victim, the innocent one who goes to the grave with every victim of injustice. He hangs there for, and with, every innocent: victims of exploitation, slaves, children shot in school, executives ripped by car bombs, workers brought low by chemicals, women sold into prostitution, bystanders in war—all of them, without exception, hang on the Cross. But not only victims. The victimizers, the oppressors, the guilty: the Cross is for them too.

See it from above. As the fathers of Vatican II wrote, by his incarnation the Son of God has in a sense united himself with every human being (*Gaudium et Spes,* 22). If that

· · · · · ·

is true, then an astonishing corollary follows. When we see Jesus, we see true humanity. It is you and I, guilty and innocent, *every human person*, who hangs on that judge's beam, that Cross. Not in torturous pain, but in our true humanity, our authentic selves. On this day we have been lifted up with him in his salvation of the world. For that reason also, we call this Friday good.

THE GREAT VIGIL OF EASTER is the mother of all liturgies. If you live in a parish where the Vigil is kept, you will experience, through word and light and sacrament, the entire sweep of our salvation. First there are the ancient stories of creation, deliverance, and promise; then Christ's passage from death to life, symbolized by the imposition of the water of baptism; and finally the bread and the wine, served to us miraculously from the other side of the grave. All this, done with dramatic actions: the darkness is first broken by a single candle, then illumined by many candles, and finally ablaze with all light; the silence is first broken by the human voice, till by the end, all the bells in the church sing out (and at Resurrection we tell everyone to bring bells with them); color is suddenly exposed in flower and tapestry when the purple coverings are ripped away. The Easter Vigil is, indeed, the mother of every other liturgy. In fact, everything the church does through the year is actually a repetition of a portion of the Great Vigil. In the Daily Office we re-read, methodically and carefully, the salvation story. Baptism, at any time, ties us into the paschal reality celebrated at the Vigil. And our weekly Eucharist reminds us that every Sunday is, in a sense, Easter.

The Vigil is properly celebrated through the night, though these days we must often make compromises. In some places, for example, concerns about crime require that the Vigil be held early in the evening. Others, however, such as Resurrection in its semi-suburban setting, can keep the Vigil in the middle of the night; and that has been a great blessing for me. And, contrary to what one might expect, having a church service in the middle of the night does not mean we lack young people. Eight teenaged acolytes support me in the liturgy. And young children come in pajamas with their pillows and blankets, sacking out wherever they like: on a pew, in a corner, or downstairs in the undercroft.

One year, after renewing our baptismal vows, everyone took their candles and processed outside to our cemetery. We were chanting a litany of the saints, and it was just past midnight. Not yet had we said the A-word (which, of course, hadn't been said since Shrove Tuesday). After a prayer for the departed, I looked at about a hundred beatific faces, lit with the candles they were nursing in their hands. (Nothing is as beautiful as the human face lit by a candle. As the priest, I have the best view!) I smiled. "Are you ready?" I asked. Then the shout: ALLELUIA. And everyone cried out, "Alleluia. Christ is risen." We began to ring the bells. Our church bell pealed. The bells sang through the night, a noisy accompaniment to the Orthodox hymn, "Christ is risen from the dead, trampling down death by death." As we reentered the church in all this joyous clamoring, there, under the balcony, in the midst of all the jingle bells and cow bells and the church bell and the singing, we found Nicholas, in his Power Ranger sleeping bag, sound asleep, watched over by his father.

This year Joey, age five, came in his pajamas. He sat on the kneeler, his coloring-book on the pew bench. When all the lights went out at the start of the Vigil, he discovered that his pajamas glowed in the dark. This was cool, and he let his mother know it. "Shshsh," she said. Then Joey saw, projected on the back wall of the church, sharp shadows created by the new fire. He could not see the fire, only the shadows, and when the thurible opened, Joey saw the opening jaws of a monster. "Monster!" he cried, point-

· · · · · ·

ing. Apparently monsters are a big thing in Joey's life. When incense was placed into the thurible, Joey saw something going into the mouth of the monster. He was quite excited. Then time passed, and Joey settled down to focus on the candle in his hand. After the Exsultet, he seemed to be falling asleep, and his mother took the candle away. But never underestimate the power of a child's attention. The lector was reading the six days of creation from Genesis 1, when she said, "And God made the sea-monsters." Joey came alive. "Mommy, God made the sea-monsters!" It was a theological insight, a real linking of his imaginary and religious worlds.

Joy permeates the whole evening. Holy Saturday begins with an ecumenical morning service, followed by a rehearsal for the acolytes and lay readers. Others put out tulips and hyacinths and polish every square inch of metal, while the choir goes over the music one last time. A few quiet hours in the afternoon follow the bustle of our preparations.

We begin the service at 10:30 P.M., and often I am not home from the party until past 3 A.M. What happens on Easter Day? I'm not really sure. I'm there, I celebrate the Eucharist, and those who come who haven't been to church for a year tell me they find it a beautiful service. But my heart is in the Vigil, the mother of all liturgies.

. . . . . .

# Kay

. . . . .

KAY HAD COME TO OUR PARISH from the Bronx, but she was born in Jamaica, and Jamaica always remained her home. After a few years with us, her cancer was discovered, and she went through about three years of intermittent treatments. I had always known her as a thin, beautiful woman with a pious dignity. Towards the end, she managed to find the strength to take a final trip to Jamaica. Shortly after she returned, I took her Communion.

While I was visiting, she showed me a precious book. It was a very large, very old Bible that had been in her family for many years, and which she had brought back with her. She tenderly unwrapped it. The covers were loose, as were many of the pages. It had suffered water damage in the recent hurricane; the pages were mildewed and stained. No matter how carefully we lifted them, the pages fell apart in our fingers. It was a large Bible, several inches thick. As we lifted its leaves, Kay and I thought about the generations of faithful people who had read this book and been touched by the words in it.

Today I think of the frail woman standing at her kitchen counter, gently lifting the crumbling pages of the old Bible. What is important with a Bible is not the strength of its spine, or the weight of its paper, or the quality of its ink, but the Word that is written in it. And what was important with Kay was not the strength of her spine, or the weight of her body, or the quality of her mind, but the Word which, through baptism and Communion, put the seal of the Cross on her heart.

. . . . .

Sometimes an old Bible is in such bad shape that there is nothing you can do but copy out the family tree and bury the book in the ground. Yet while we may bury a Bible, we do not lose the Word of God. Kay's body has gone to the grave, but the Word of the Lord lives forever, and in that Word Kay, and I, and perhaps you, have placed our hope.

. . . . . .

# The Burial of the Dead

WHEN PRINCESS DIANA DIED, I was moved to say something critical, not of her, but of the living. It was hard to watch the British people deconstruct their legendary sense of reserve. You probably recall the scene (although, with the passage of only a few years, the details now feel surrealistic). The throngs of people, the piles of flowers, the leather-bound books for them to write messages of condolence. First there were, I believe, two books, then six, then forty-seven—an official explained that there wasn't room for more than forty-seven—and people were standing in line for ten hours, maybe more, to write in these books. To write what? To be read by whom? And we were notified that plans were in place to remove the flowers with great care, removing every tag and card so that they could be remembered. The royal family was bitterly criticized because they hadn't put their grief over the airwaves for all of us to see and gape and "share." When I first read about all these British goings-on, I thought, "My God, they've become Americans."

Now that the British have lost their reserve there is, it seems to me, just one place where reserve still exists, and it is a place worth maintaining. And that's in the burial rite of the Book of Common Prayer. This is a masterpiece of reserve. Indeed, it seems that from 1552 to 1662 the Anglican rite for the Burial of the Dead often came at the end of Evensong. With remarkable simplicity and ordinariness, at the end of the daily service that closed the workday, the congregation would process out into the churchyard where a few additional prayers would be said before the body was lowered into the ground. In its subsequent revisions, there remained at most only one thing that was said about the deceased: his or her *name*, the Christian name, the name pronounced at baptism. Nothing else: no eulogy, no extra talk. We are all equal in death.

This is a principle worth maintaining, and my mentor, Father Michael Webber who used to be rector at Zion Church in Wappingers Falls, New York, liked to say that if anyone dared to speak one word about him at his funeral, he was going to rise up out of the coffin and shoot the malefactor. I urge you to make similar burial instructions. And while you're at it, you might specify that you want a cheap coffin. The body of Princess Diana was brought back to England in a simple pine box, covered with the royal standard. A church customarily has a pall, and everyone buried from the parish will be covered by it.

We are all equal in death, and our equality is precisely our baptismal gift: equality as children of God. This equality is what is proclaimed when we approach death with Prayer Book reserve. What is important about any of us is not those endowments that we make so much of—physical beauty, brains, grace, or cleverness. The problem with funeral eulogies is that it is so hard to speak the truth about the deceased. And yet there is no moment in life where it is more important that we speak the truth than when we face death. When I die, please just speak my name in the holy place and leave me to God.

. . . . . .

THAT JUNE, two things happened. Susan turned thirty-eight, and she was found to have a brain tumor. They gave her steroids to keep it from pressing too much on her brain until the surgery could be performed. Those were long weeks. The drugs made her puffy and tired. Her mother had flown out from New Mexico to help a little; she liked to take her walking in the cool evenings. Her mother was good at walks and at most practical things, but had rejected all religion, and so knew none of the comforts of prayer. Unlike, everyone thought, us. It was one of our dry summers, and by early July the grass was only tiny sticks and dust.

We sat on the sofa watching our children play on the yard. They were nine and thirteen then, and although we had withheld nothing from them, their child-hearts could entertain no tragic thoughts. Mama had a brain tumor; she was going to have surgery; she would get better. We marveled at their love for play.

Across the yard from the rectory we could see the church. Everyone was praying for her, and being helpful as only a parish can be, with daily offerings of food, car rides, cards, letters. So many cards and letters! Every day the mail brought more, and every one of them brightly said, "We're praying for you." Some were humorous; some sentimental; many "religious." But always, behind the various flowers and pictures and icons, were a hundred attestations of prayer and spiritual support.

And as we watched our children, she said to me: "None of this makes any sense any more. I feel my mother's concern, I see our children's love, I read all these cards. And I can't pray."

She was in the center of prayer, and yet prayer was for her as distant as the planet Pluto, as inaccessible as quantum physics. The inaccessibility of prayer was totally unexpected, like having a five-star gourmet dinner delivered to your door but finding (or feeling) that your nose no longer smelled and your tongue no longer tasted and, worst of all, your body no longer took in food.

Prayer no longer made sense. It made no intellectual sense, for she couldn't figure out what it was supposed to do. And it made no affective sense. She felt simply but utterly disconnected. "I understand the externals. I see the exteriors. But I can't pray."

Should she have forced herself upon prayer, summoned up her spiritual resources by sheer will power and made herself pray? I don't think so. Embedded in Eastern Orthodox spirituality is a sense of the community's prayers being strong enough to carry along the individual. Each individual worshiper doesn't need to pay attention or be focused throughout the entire liturgy: for God has so arranged it that at any given time at least one person is genuinely praying. In one of his visits to the patriarch in Moscow, Bishop Grein attended an ordination service at a Moscow cathedral. He was late arriving, and as he entered he passed a man, vested, smoking a cigarette. "Are you serving in the liturgy?" the bishop asked. "No," he answered, "I'm getting ordained."

Something like this, standing outside, aware of the incense and chant and beauty inside but unable to be in there, happened to her in those dry summer days. She was the focus of intense spiritual energy and yet felt utterly alien to it. Months later, after her surgery, she told me that it was the signal experience of her illness, a spiritual lesson she will never forget. To be surrounded by prayer, and unable to pray—it was, she said, an experience of church.

. . . . . .

MY DAUGHTER AND I were in Wellfleet, a little village on Cape Cod, walking in the early fall afternoon through galleries not yet shuttered for the winter. I am always hopeful that amongst works amateurish, bizarre, or simply dull, I will discover a beautiful thing that speaks to me. And even if that doesn't happen, just the walking and exploring is pleasant.

So we were not looking for anything in particular. One shop selling note cards, paintings, and small handcrafted objects was giving out hot apple cider, the first cider of the fall. In the next gallery we passed little clay people in whimsical poses. They were seated on ledges or lined along the baseboards in every room, and they made us chuckle. We moved further into this gallery, made a couple of turns, and found the treasure we had been looking for all along without knowing it. It was a small thing, easily overlooked—a tempera painting, maybe eight-inches-by-twelve, in a mahogany frame. This painting showed a hallway: wooden floor, rich dark walls, passages to either side, a window straight ahead. White wood crisscrossed the windowpanes into small squares. A garden lay beyond the window, empty like the hall itself, of human or animal life, but warm with friendly sunlight. I wanted to step in and sit by that window with a favorite novel and sip afternoon tea.

All this was done with uncommon precision, a style utterly transparent to its object. My daughter noted the magic of it: the wood of the walls and the floor was as vibrant as the mahogany of the frame. Nothing outside a museum had ever before struck me as so perfectly crafted. In short, I felt awe, and I was ready to worship.

I knelt to see the price. In four digits, it was far beyond anything I could afford. Yet I started to wonder: maybe I could find a way to buy it? (What's a year of college tuition anyway?) Indeed, that evening, I found myself—in the last idle moments before falling asleep—mentally calculating arrangements that I might be able to make. I could persuade Emily she didn't need college. I could cash in my life insurance. . . . I felt like the merchant who, after discovering the pearl of great price, put it back where he found it, and then went to sell all.

In the event, however, I didn't sell all, and I left the painting behind. But just as the parable was not about the pearl, this encounter was not about the painting. I probably meet someone every day who is as unexpected and beautiful as that painting. They contain rooms and side passages that I can only glimpse. They open up beyond themselves to a vision—*their* vision—of a garden (and the garden suggests paradise). And if I glimpse one of them for who she really is, I want to come in and have some tea (and the tea suggests communion). My daily problem is that I don't see. Regarding most people, I am only half-awake. But what I do see in certain people (my daughter, my wife, my friend) is what God sees in, what is true of, every person. Something unexpected. Something worthy of worship. Something for which I would give all.

. . . . . .

# An Upper Room

· · · · · ·

IT WAS, SOMEONE SAID, a conference schedule designed by theological Nazis. We had started at 8:30. Yes, A.M. The day had included six serious theological lectures on the Nicene Creed, punctuated only by short breaks (and this was but day two of four). Even lunch was covered: we were to have a roundtable discussion of the lectures we heard the day before. By evening our brains were limp dishrags. Eight of us migrated, raucously, to a local restaurant. Two hours and three leisurely courses later, a couple of us wanted cigars.

That led to about a mile's worth of walking, until finally we stumbled upon the destination. It was an unusual establishment. Two facing walls, the center island, and the front window—all filled with shelves upon shelves of cigars with exotic names. I had never seen so many cigars before. These cigars were aspiring to the self-importance of fine wines. I learned that you buy your cigar downstairs (with the expert advice of the proprietor) and then ascend a circular staircase to an upper room. There, on divans that could just as well grace an opium den, you stretch your limbs and light up. A fetching young woman offers a port list; in honor of the theologian, I chose a Macquarrie's.

We were friends relaxing together after a long day. In part, friends celebrate the simple fact of the day being accomplished: we got through it, and we're done until tomorrow, hallelujah. Friends also become less restrained. Things, which in the decorum of daylight would not be said, now become sayable. There is some appropriate ribbing and teasing, and with it, perhaps, a bit of soul-exposure.

· · · · · ·

Since we were all theologians, we lifted our glasses in a toast to Athanasius. "*Contra mundum!*" we said—against the world! Then someone said it was time for retractions. What theological positions have you held in the past that you now are willing to retract? The discussion circled the room, bringing gravity to our light-headedness. I confessed that I was once quite enamored of process theology. The response was unanimous incredulity. "You, Victor, a process theologian?" (To claim an affection for process theology among my friends is like supporting the death penalty among Quakers.) It was, I owned, a shameful part of my past. And yet I wasn't ready to renounce it altogether.

After an hour or so—for the record, it takes longer to smoke a cigar than to sip a glass of port—we descended to the darkened street and walked back to the hotel. We broke into smaller groups, and I found myself pausing at my room door, having a final short talk with one of the others. Acknowledging the late hour and the fullness of the day, he stopped to ask me what I was most grateful for in the day and what I most regretted; "You know," he said, "that quasi-Ignatian exercise for the end of the day." We were tired enough, and had laughed enough, that suddenly a deep seriousness fell over us. I don't remember my answer, but I remember his. It came out slowly and thoughtfully. "I am grateful for a day with people I love." And regrets? "I was a little too cynical, but not so much as I might have been."

As I turned into my room, I felt I was unworthy of such an intense and rich day as this had been. We had studied theology through the day, and shared friendship in the evening. Perhaps a test of true theology is its ability to form friendships. Jesus Christ, on the most remembered night of history, gathered his disciples in an upper room. And in that upper room he also made a point of saying to them: "I have called you friends."

· · · · · ·

# Theologian and Parish Priest

I AM A THEOLOGIAN and a parish priest. This combination may be unusual in the contemporary world. Yet I would argue that any division between theology and pastoral practice is artificial, probably a result of a misconceived notion of professionalism, and certainly unnecessary. My parishioners, of whatever intellectual achievements, constantly bring up real theological questions. I believe that the most important pastoral task is to provide places and opportunities where *real questions*, questions that ordinary people have, *can be asked and addressed*. They don't find me "unpastoral" as a result; rather, they tend to find it refreshing.

"Father," one says, "if we didn't have the Bible, would we know that there is a god?"

"We could figure it out," I say. Philosophers have four basic ways of showing that God exists. Some, like the great Archbishop of Canterbury, St. Anselm, say that there is something unique about the very question of God's existence: if we are able to ask it, then he must exist. I don't quite accept this argument, although, I have to say, there was what happened to Carol. Carol was a year ahead of me at college, and one day I happened to run into her as I was doing my laundry. "It's true, Victor!" she exclaimed, her copy of Anselm in her hands. "What's true?" I asked. "God exists!" she shouted. Reading Anselm changed Carol's life.

Of the other ways of showing God's existence, one is based on mystical experience, another on the evidence that this universe has been designed, and the third, the one I personally find most compelling, on the sheer fact that there is a world rather than nothing. "How come anything at all?" is how my teacher paraphrased Aquinas's question. For anything to happen, there has to be a cause, and then the cause needs a cause, and so on. But the whole chain of causes also has to have a cause, a cause that is not itself caused, and that is what we mean when we say "God."

"But, Father, that's not what I mean when I say God. I mean someone who knows me and loves me."

"Good point: philosophy only takes us so far." The arguments that God exists don't tell us anything about God's character. "But weren't you telling me a few weeks ago that your son asked you, 'If God made everything, who made God?' It's very natural to ask that question. Human thought cannot avoid pushing up against this chain-of-causes argument. Here's an answer you can try out: what it means to be God is that God is the one and only being in the universe you cannot ask, 'Who made you?' Because if God had a maker, then the maker would be the real God."

I have a question time after my sermons, which we place at the end of the Sunday liturgy (they run concurrently with church school classes; it's a space-limitation thing—the space for church school is also the space for coffee hour). Lots of the questions that come up are about free will. Many people distinguish between the things that God causes, and the things that happen by our free agency. Suppose there is a man named George, and suppose that George suddenly dies. If no one can identify the cause, some people attribute his death to God. But then you see the bullet wound in George's chest, and you see the gun in my hand. You change your mind: "*God* didn't cause George's death; *Victor* did."

Sounds logical enough, but actually there's a big problem here. It's that this line of thought treats God as if he were another element of the universe, an actor like you and me only more powerful and invisible. But God is not *something*, for then (to repeat something I said before) he would be just another cause in the chain of causes, and, being *something* he would himself need a cause of his existence.

"Now Father, how can you say God exists but he isn't something?"

"It's very paradoxical, but he exists because he is God, and he isn't something because he is God." And if God is not a thing among things, then we must revisit that customary distinction between events brought about by God and events brought about by free human agency. It is better, I have come to believe, to recognize God as the cause of everything that happens, *absolutely everything*. But if you are considering two events—the fall of a rock, for instance, and the production of a symphony—it is in the event in which human freedom is *most* present that God's causal activity is also *most* evident. God acts most clearly in our own free acts. This leaves us with the problem of dear dead George: now his death is caused by God, no matter what. But the flip side is an amazing truth. When I act freely and creatively, God is most especially the cause of what I do!

FOR SEVERAL YEARS our Sunday school students sponsored, through fund-raisers, some children who had been orphaned in Ethiopia. In return we received general letters about the schools and homes where these children lived. One year we learned how they keep Christmas. It goes like this. After a six-week fast, on Christmas Eve they go to church. A vigil of prayer and fasting is kept through the night until 9 or 10 the next morning. Then comes the leisurely beautiful Ethiopian Orthodox liturgy. Since Christmas is not a public holiday in Ethiopia, most people have to go to work; nonetheless, the churches are full, so full that the crowds overflow onto the grounds outside.

After the liturgy there is great feasting. Ethiopians do not have our customs of the crèche, the tree, and the exchange of presents. Instead, they have a traditional coffee ceremony, and a traditional game, called "gena" (which means "nativity"), which was described to us as "a fast and furious game played by men on horseback." This game is apparently a cross between hockey and polo. The men hit a wooden ball with sticks, "galloping up and down at a great speed, trying to score a goal. The children take it up and everywhere there are bands of small boys going off into the woods to cut sticks for themselves and with a makeshift ball, imitating their elders until sunset makes it too dark to play."[*]

When I think about men on horseback racing through villages, trying to hit a wooden ball with sticks as they race and hope to score a goal, in a game which is named

---

[*]Quotations are from a report by Ms. Gil Elers, volunteer from St. Matthew's Children's Fund, U.K.

"nativity," I realize that Christmas could be quite different than we Americans have it. Instead of gorging ourselves for weeks, we could fast, and it would still be Christmas. It could be a workday, and still be Christmas. We could have church mid-morning, rather than midnight, and still it would be Christmas. We could watch men on horseback in the streets, instead of football on television. And perhaps hardest to imagine of all, there could be no presents, no tree, no Christmas shopping season—and it would still be Christmas.

Imagine going home after midnight mass, unlocking your door, flipping the light— and nothing happens. You grope your way to a closet and feel for a flashlight; thank God, it works. You look around, your eyes following the narrow cone of dim light, and turn the corner into your living room. When you left to come to church a few hours ago, you had a small mountain of brightly colored boxes stacked under the tree. They are gone. The tree itself is gone; the ornaments, lights, all gone. There is no sign of violence or mayhem, no broken glass, no damage to the door, no (come to think of it) little dry evergreen needles on the carpet. You stop and listen as hard as you can and hear nothing—not even the sound of the refrigerator. You rush back to the kitchen: at least that's still there, but you open it, and shine in the light. The milk and the cheese and the ketchup and all the other ordinary refrigerator litter is there, but the Christmas goose, the Christmas dinner, is gone. Someone has come into your house and removed every trace of Christmas.

Sitting down now, your flashlight beside you (turned off to save the batteries), leaning on the Formica of the kitchen table, your mind turns to places you have seen in your life. You think of them, in a kind of video fast-forward, as they change through time. You watch as skyscrapers grow over New York City, they shine, then they age, then they blur and are gone. Waves lap the shore of a bare Manhattan Island. You think of Jones beach, or it may be Rhode Island, or Cape Cod, or Lake Michigan: on a sunshiny day, crowds frolicking, you are there and yet you are also watching, and again the vision flickers—and they are gone. Waves lap deserted sands. You go to your high school: you see it built, you see children come and go, you see flags raised and lowered, and then—as with the beach, as with the city—the image dissolves, leaving only rock, rubble, and weeds.

And you think of St. John's Christmas words. *In the beginning was the Word. . . . And the Word became flesh and dwelt among us.* You think of births you have seen, births you awaited, the pain, the blood, the cry; the joy of the first smile, the first words, the hugs; you think of pimples, and dates, and discovery, and hard labor, and conflict. You remember the room where you first saw death, the human hand strangely cold, the chest no longer to rise and fall but forever still.

Again: *In the beginning was the Word. . . . And the Word was made flesh and dwelt among us.* You remember those moments when your friend smiled at you, holding a candle in your hand; you remember the long walk, the prayers, the stumbling, the sore feet, the cries, palm branches, a donkey, a blanket, a cup, a race, confusion, shouting, "Crucify!", darkness.

*And the light shines on in the darkness, and the darkness has never mastered it.* You sit in your strangely empty house. Is this still Christmas? And just then you taste (or is it the remembrance of a taste?) bread on your tongue; you smell the wine on your lips. *The Word became flesh.* The sun rises, your doorbell rings.

. . . . . .

# Café
. . . . .

HALF-DOZEN YEARS AGO, when I started commuting to school in the Bronx, the natives came forth with useful advice: how to drive there, where to park, what to look for. The best advice was culinary. Fordham, they explained, is right on the edge of Little Italy. And Little Italy is where you find Arthur Avenue. More than one person told me, "You must go get bread from Arthur Avenue."

It wasn't long before I had made the acquaintance of Arthur Avenue bakeries; a few years later, a friend routinely suggested Italian coffee and something sweet. We'd leave the library, exit through the iron gates, and after a few blocks' walk settle into our favorite place. Espresso and canoli: everything you need to talk theology.

Then Little Italy came to the hamlet where I live, some sixty miles north of the Bronx.

Mario's "brick oven" bakery opened quietly, hidden behind the optometrist's shop and the State Farm agent. You could go there and buy *pane di casa*, or long French sticks, or rolls. Ask for a dozen, and you were likely to get seventeen. Retail exactitude was clearly not their main business. They supplied restaurants all over the county. One day I saw a truck delivering flour. I asked, "How much flour do you use, Mario?" About ten bags. "How much is in a bag?" A hundred pounds! "Every week?" Every day!

Business was good, and so, after a few years, Mario expanded. With the help of a couple of other entrepreneurs (all of whom speak fluent Italian), Café Tiramisu appeared on our main drag, between a deli and a laundromat. A light, airy storefront with small

. . . . . .

tables and metal-backed chairs, Café Tiramasu is actually three culinary centers combined. To the right as you enter, along the wall, are Mario's authentic breads. There's gourmet pizza in the back, where frantic fellows grab telephones, scribble orders, twirl dough, chop, pour, arrange, and cook the pizzas that they slide in and out of their large ovens. And in front of the breads are glass cases, filled with a range of Italian pastries, pies, and cakes.

I tell everyone about Café Tiramasu—family, parishioners, visitors, and my fellow students at Fordham. With the exaggeration of a true fan, I pronounce it to be the best thing to have happened to our hamlet in years. You can go in there, order cappuccino and a Napoleon, take a seat, pull out a book, and no one will bother you. Or if your daughter missed lunch, you can drop in and get a spinach calzone at three in the afternoon. You can linger and observe the people who come and go. Or, when time is short, you can be yourself someone who comes and goes, grabbing four dozen hard rolls for a parish dinner.

Places like this little café with its distinctive character are important for community life. Where I live, everyone has to have a car. It's not a small town; it's a development of developments. You drive to soccer. You drive to church. Our church is located amidst private homes. You drive three-quarters of a mile along a state highway without sidewalks to get from us to the town hall and library. By design, there are no connecting back roads. No building is centrally located, and there is no town square where people can gather.

Yet now we have this little place where you can drop in, visit or be alone, listen to Sicilian accents, and eat good food. It all started with bread—substantial, earthly bread.

. . . . . .

And it strikes me that this is the sort of rooted, particular place that Christians should cultivate. For although we are on our way to a heavenly city, we have a divinely mandated concern to make the earthly city as humane as possible. We need to be concerned, for instance, about the effects of automobile-dependency upon human community, how when we drive everywhere we have fewer opportunities to meet and sit with each other. We need to celebrate the occasions where the good and the beautiful flourish. Here is a bread shop that I can celebrate, and perhaps even recall that one of the names for my Lord is the Bread of the World.

OUR PARISH IS IN THE HUDSON VALLEY in New York. That means taxes are high and winters are cold—not cold, mind you, by any serious standard; we do not get "snow upon snow" which piles higher and higher. Which is to say, we aren't Minnesota. Nor are our taxes as high as those in most European countries. Nonetheless, the perception amongst the natives is that we have heavy taxes and taxing winters, and, as they say, "the natives are restless."

They show their restlessness, first, by taking short sorties into foreign lands. Shaking my hand after services, one of them will say, "Father, you won't see me for two weeks; I'm going off to visit my cousin in Florida." It always starts like that: the trip is "justified" by the existence of a relative. Never mind that the relative is a seventh cousin thrice removed; the cousin needs a visit particularly during the month of February, which I'm told is a difficult month for residents of Florida.

The second phase arrives when our explorers return and start speaking of the warmer and less taxing clime as the land of milk and honey. "I went swimming in the ocean last week," one will say as, shaking my hand at the end of services, we view the snow falling outdoors.

"I hope the water didn't scald you," I reply. "I hear the water is very warm in Florida."

"Oh, not at this time of year, Father," she will say.

"And how were the snakes," I ask, forcing a smile. "Did you see many?"

· · · · · ·

The third phase is a mollifying one. "This time, Father," she says, "I brought back some church bulletins for you. They have very active Episcopal churches down there: large congregations, programs all week, outreach programs. I think you'll be impressed." I try to look grateful for the literature. "Do you want this back when I'm done?" I always ask. They never do.

The fourth phase has arrived when you start learning more than you ever wanted to know about Florida real estate. "Father, I would be able to buy two homes down there for the price of mine up here. And I'd be paying less in taxes." I try to remind her about the snakes, but I know I've lost the battle.

It is a cliché to say that ours is a mobile society. And I am no domestic purist: I live fifteen hundred miles from my parents, two thousand miles from my brother, and two thousand miles from most of my wife's sisters. I grew up in Oklahoma, went to college, got married, and taught school in New Mexico, then I came to New York for seminary and have lived in the Hudson Valley since. In our society, we tend to live where we choose to live—for vocational reasons, for the local culture, for economy, or even for the climate. The result often puts great distance between ourselves and our extended families.

Yet I am a parish priest, given the sacred trust of summoning together a community of faith in order that we may be God's people in this place and do God's work here. And it is hard on the priestly soul to have parishioners—faithful, hardworking folk who have matured in faith, people I have seen draw closer to the Lord and whose gifts I have had a little hand in drawing out—reach a certain age and suddenly decide they are going to move away from their community of thirty or forty or even fifty years in order to live

. . . . . .

among strangers for their remaining days. They will (I'm sure) make new friends, and they will be welcome assets for their new churches. But I can't help but wonder if we are wise to shed a community so easily, so often?

Of course, in the end we are all temporary sojourners on this earth, pilgrims passing through. But to say that is to point out how a voluntary move for the sake of physical comfort is akin to a voluntary, chosen death—like choosing to leave this life for the life to come. I will admit that it is possible (if far-fetched) that God calls some northeasterners to retire and move away. Even so, however, it always hurts—it's a little like death.

IT IS THE SUDDENNESS OF A MIRACLE, which, as much as anything, commands our attention. The man was lame; Jesus said, "Rise, go." The man got up and walked. A woman had been bleeding for years; she touched Jesus' garment; the flow of blood ceased. A miracle, so it seems, comes not only in the transformation of infirmity into health but also in the speed of the transition. At once, in an instant: *that's* a miracle.

But is a miracle in fact always a simple, abrupt event? Lest we think so, Mark 8:22–26 records an unusual case in which the healing occurred in stages. A blind man was brought to Jesus. Jesus took him by the hand and led him off alone. He put spit upon his eyes; laid his hands upon them. He asked the man what he saw. And the man who had been blind said, "I see men as trees, walking." Jesus put his hands on the man's eyes again. Then the healing was complete and the man could see clearly.

The man was healed in a process. And in the midst of the process he had to answer a question. For people who seek to reinvigorate the church's healing ministry today, this is a very important passage. You may be praying for someone who is ill. You may be laying your hands upon her as you pray. It is also undeniably permitted, and may in fact be advisable, for you to pause in your prayers to ask the person what she is feeling. Does she sense any change happening? What is she seeing?

And by pausing to ask a question, the person who would be healed is required to be self-aware. "I see men as trees, walking," the man says. His blindness is departing, and he reports that he has vision of sorts. He must admit that some healing has occurred, yet also own that the healing process is not yet complete. In this way, by means of his honesty combined with his faith, the man cooperates with his healing.

And cooperation generates hope. I have prayed with and for a number of people who, following the imposition of hands, were indeed healed. Even though their improvement could be attributed to other causes—a natural reversal of the course of the illness, or a response to medical therapy—these people believe that God miraculously healed them. But they are few. By far the greater number that I pray for do not experience restored health. They may be partially healed. Or they may be spiritually strengthened even as their body continues to decline. Their healing is a process that involves many dimensions. They may say, "I see men as trees, walking."

And is it possible that, at the mid-stage of the process, there was a gift of spiritual insight, that before the blind man received physical sight, his spiritual sight was restored? Spiritual blindness, after all, is much more common than the physical sort. Most of us, most of the time, are blind to the realities of the human lives around us. The people whose paths cross ours—the drivers in the other cars, the clerks and shopkeepers, the voices of customer service—all these people might just as well be trees that happen to walk or talk. We too, in our non-sensitivity, might be closer to a walking tree than we would like to think.

Could it be that the blind man had his truest sight not at the end of the healing process, when he had received conventional vision, but in the middle, when he looked at us and saw "trees, walking"? Perhaps healing is about what happens in the midst of the process, when we come to see a spiritual truth about ourselves and our human race. Maybe the man in the story saw most truly not at the end but in the middle—maybe then he saw our customary inhuman humanity.

. . . . .

# Face It

· · · · · ·

"GOD INTENDS to kill us, and in the end he will succeed." That was my philosophy. I had seen evidence: I could think of dozens of people who had something precious ripped away, just at the moment they realized the preciousness. I remember, for instance, a young man who had looked down upon his grandfather as a person of a distant age, with vastly different—and inferior—interests from his own. Just after leaving college, he found he had finally reached an age where he could appreciate his grandfather—and just then the old man was diagnosed with cancer. In four months he was dead. He had just started to value him, to look up to him, and he was gone.

"Just when you start to appreciate something, God will take it away." That's what I said. I also pointed to nature for evidence: God has intertwined beauty and transience. Today a rose is fresh and alert, all the petals stand at attention, separated from one another just enough to release the perfect scent hidden inside. Tomorrow the petals curl backwards, like limp dancers; the next day their edges are brown; soon there's only dry dust to be wiped off the table.

"Face it," I said, "God's design for us is to remove everything we love or find beautiful." I drew evidence even from Scripture. Anything we attempt to idolize, God will take away (for our own good, of course). So if money becomes an idol, the hand of God may strike us in the bankruptcy court. If we over-prize our good looks, God will let us age. If we trust in our own strength, God will . . . kill us.

My spiritual director said, "Do I sense a rather negative picture of God?" And he wisely took God's part and began a dialogue with me.

· · · · · ·

"I see that you think I do everything I can to frustrate people," he said.

"You do have a reputation for bringing harm. You killed your own son." I had a point to make here.

"Are you forgetting the role of free will?"

"You mean, you didn't do it, but Judas did? That won't wash, because free will, if it's free, is your creation too. You act *in* my freedom, not around it."

"True. But what do you say about Moses?"

"That he grew up in a cruel world? That you wouldn't leave him alone? That he never got to enter the Promised Land?" My voice had an acid edge.

"Not that he saw my face?"

"So you're saying, everything else is acceptable, provided a person gets to see your face?"

I stopped . . . listening to the words that came out of my mouth. The question to which my spiritual director drew me was its own answer. Not the cruel philosophy that everything is "acceptable," that is, that somehow evil and pain will turn out not to have been so bad. Rather a more loving philosophy that everything can be accepted, taken in, and given some kind of shelter in our soul, if we have what my spiritual director calls "a relationship with God." I'm not sure what sense to make of that phrase, since God is not in any sense something else, someone else, among the creatures of this world. Nonetheless, I know what it means. Shortly after this dialogue, at the end of a day of solitary retreat, I had the unmistakable experience in prayer of seeing eyes looking at me. Just eyes. I could not see beyond the eyes, but I knew that I was being seen. Seen, and seen through, and understood. It is said that the profoundest human longing is to be seen by another. Those eyes may still intend to kill me, yet I would easily give my life for such eyes.

. . . . . .

I TEACH A COURSE IN ETHICS to college students. Because this is a required course, my students represent a cross-section of all the disciplines at Marist College. And their diversity—from criminal justice to social work to computers to fashion—makes our discussions lively. Yet, however diverse their interests, they enter the class with a common presumption which is, I believe, at the heart of many evils that beset our culture today. Along with virtually everybody, they simply assume that freedom and obedience are opposites; that freedom is increased when choices are increased; and, with regard to ethics, that what is morally right or wrong depends upon the choice of each individual person.

I do an informal poll at the beginning of each course. "When you think of ethics," I ask, "what comes to mind?" The last time I asked, out of a class of thirteen, everyone named an issue. One named cloning, one named environmental preservation, one named genetic engineering, one named adultery, and one didn't know. Eight named abortion.

The abortion debate is the common paradigm of an ethical issue, and how is the issue framed in our culture? As an issue of individual rights, of personal decision, a matter of private choice. The opposing camps will argue about who the individuals involved really are, or about what decision ought to be made, or who has the right to make the choice: but they do not dispute the framework within which the issue is to be discussed—a framework where freedom means choice.

I notice that an increasing number of public issues are being framed as issues of private choice. The question of tax dollars going to private schools through vouchers, for instance, is described as one form of "school choice." The question of government welfare funds going through religiously sponsored charitable organizations is called "charitable choice." Freedom in our culture is traded in the currency of "choice."

At the same time my students are equally certain of a second fact about freedom: a person can lose it by making bad choices. I ask them to consider the choice of whether to take drugs. The initial choice, perhaps, is a free one. If, however, you choose to consume an addictive substance, it may be your last free choice. On the other hand, if you consider taking on a harmful addiction but decide not to, the next time the choice presents itself you will find it easier to resist, because you now have a history of resisting. You have attained a higher degree of freedom in which you have fewer "live" choices.

The paradox is: precisely because you are less likely to choose the drug, you become more free. In this case, there is an inverse relation between the power of choice and the degree of freedom. The less pressing the choice of taking a drug, the more freedom. And the choice of taking a drug is a paradigm for any morally wrong choice.

My students are capable of seeing freedom both as the choosing between alternatives and as a quality of a person's character. I try to get them to see the contradiction in holding both views at once, and I hope they come to see that it's better to have freedom as a quality of character—as a strength of soul. One of the collects in the Book of Common Prayer says: "Set us free, O God, from the bondage of our sins and give us . . . the liberty of that abundant life . . . manifested to us in . . . Jesus Christ." (Epiphany V) We can be slaves to choices, but God can make us free, giving us "the liberty of that abundant life" that we see in Christ.

. . . . . .

THE SUN WAS SHINING, there was a cool breeze, a perfect day for a hike. Our youth group chose Breakneck Ridge, a steep and clambering trail that offers a fantastic view of the majestic Hudson River Valley. It did not take long for us to realize that, against this valley, we are slight creatures. Soon we were all laboring for breath. Higher up the wind blew harder. We stopped to rest on a broad rock, to rest and drink and be cooled by the breeze.

Jason, who was taller than any of us, wondered what it would be like to be the first person to climb this valley. There wouldn't be that train over there, for instance. Soon all of us began noticing things that wouldn't have been there: lovers sunning on the rock a little below us; roads; boats in the river; the ruins of a castle on an island; beaten-down plants; broken glass on the trail; graffiti; jet exhaust lines marking the sky.

We resumed our climb, but we were still thinking backwards in time. "Early enough," Sarah said, "there wouldn't have been dirt, just rock, and the rocks would have been sharper than they are now. Probably higher."

"Of course," another added, "if we went back far enough, the mountain wouldn't exist at all—there would just be water."

During another break, one of the climbers stretched out on his back, his arm over his eyes. "Dale is really exhausted," I said.

"No," he replied, "I was just thinking about 'the vast expanse of interstellar space.'" Everyone smiled; it was our inside joke.

The reference was to Eucharistic Prayer C, in which the priest says: "At your command all things came to be: the vast expanse of interstellar space, galaxies, suns, the planets in their courses, and this fragile earth, our island home."

So we joked among ourselves, and they teased me that Prayer C was my favorite (which it was in those days). I do like the "space" images—galaxies, planets, "this fragile earth, our island home." I also like those places in life where one can reach out and feel the grand wonder of this universe, places like this one, overlooking our neighborly river. Can there be any better image of the integration of liturgy and life, than to climb a mountain and find a eucharistic prayer on the lips of a friend?

## Abram

· · · · ·

THE MAN IS OLD, his hair gray, matted, unkempt. His skin is leather, ravaged by sun and wind and time. Long ago a god had spoken to the man and had told him that he was to uproot himself and travel to a land that he would give him, a land hundreds of miles away, and that he would make him the father of nations. Well, here is the land: but where is his inheritance? His wife—she too is old—and barren. No child has been born to her. As he looks on his wife, the father of nations grieves.

Yet he keeps faith. And once again, he hears the voice of the god.

To understand what follows, we need to recall the customs of that time. Suppose that you and I are the heads of two tribes. Suppose further that we are ready to agree not to wage war upon each other. What we do not do is sign a peace treaty. Rather, we "cut a covenant."

We gather ritually mature animals: a three-year-old heifer, a three-year-old she-goat, a three-year-old ram, a turtledove, and a pigeon. We kill the animals. Then with a knife, or perhaps with an axe, we take the heifer and chop it in two, laying one half to our right, the other to our left. We do the same with the goat and the ram: half to the right, half to the left. The bird carcasses are too small to cut, so we lay them at the end on either side. Then you and I, heads of two tribes, walk between those halves of animals. Our feet are bloodied, our eyes see the carcasses, and we are saying in effect: Be it so even unto us, should we fail to keep our covenant. It was a gory sight, and it meant serious business.

· · · · ·

The god spoke again to Abram, and in obedience he took and killed the animals and laid them out as prescribed. Then he waited. He waited through the heat of the day, with nothing to do except ward off vultures. To have faith means to do a lot of waiting. The father of faith waited even as you, perhaps, have waited, through the anxious hours of a hospital corridor. The magazines lie unread, useless. Somewhere else the sharp implements are being wielded and the blood taken care of. You have said your prayers and all you can do is wait.

As did he. And after sundown, perhaps in a vision, perhaps in a dream, perhaps in reality, he looked and saw a smoking fire pot and a flaming torch move between those hacked-up animals. Once again he heard the voice of the god. The voice assured him that the land which he had come to would be given to his descendants: that he would have children, heirs beyond counting.

It was something he never saw. We call him the father of faith, as if that were an easy thing, as if "faith" were merely a five-letter word. But in reality faith is the strangest business. It's not what we expect. It's blood, and darkness, and waiting, and a voice. I feel myself to be Abram's heir particularly when as sacramental leader of the gathered ones, I break the sacrificial loaf, and wait, and call upon the Spirit to move among the broken pieces of our lives.

# Wills

ONE DAY IN SEMINARY, our professor J. Robert Wright (who was, and still is, "Father Wright" to his students and friends who love him) handed out a Xeroxed copy of the front page of his will to our medieval history class. It was, as I recall, an elaborately hand-written and ornately bordered page that, after identifying itself as the will of J. Robert Wright, stated his first bequest. He left his soul to Almighty God his maker. Though there were other bequests in the following pages, this disposition of the soul, apparently a once-customary Christian practice, was the item of first importance.

How we dispose of the things we accumulate during our lives reflects on the condition of our soul. A priest in the Episcopal Church has the duty to remind his or her people of their responsibility to make wills to provide for their families, particularly their children; remembering, so far as possible, to make charitable and religious bequests (The Book of Common Prayer, 445).

Our little parish has, in fewer than five years, grown an endowment from zero to over $65,000, largely on the basis of bequests.

What's surprising (to a materialistic mind-set) is that the size of these bequests bears almost no relationship to the wealth of the decedent. Resurrection's first gift came from a woman who was the senior member of our parish when she died. She was childless, and left ten percent of her estate to the church, a gift of nearly $10,000. Another long-time member left a generous gift of $5,000. Yet another, a housecleaner who had struggled to maintain her independence, left $12,000. God had carried her through a divorce and the death of a daughter through AIDS, and had given her strength to continue working even as her emphysema got worse. God had provided, and God was going to be thanked.

My father-in-law's will contained one of the most creative bequests I have heard of. He had been an amateur painter, and his house and its outbuildings were filled with watercolors, oils, and ink drawings. His estate was very modest, and he left it all, apart from his paintings, to his wife. She was to receive certain ones that he specified. The rest went to his five daughters, who were to divide them according to a procedure he laid out. They were to gather, and then, starting with the eldest, each was to pick one painting; and they were to continue cycling through the five of them until all the paintings had been divided.

The five sisters lived in California, Colorado, New Mexico, and New York—just getting them back to the house in the New Mexico mountains all at once took two years. All of us were apprehensive, fearing that the experience would be filled with tension and argument. No one knew how many paintings there were, but it seemed likely there would be several hundred. When they got together, the sisters took all the paintings to an empty house next door and shut out husbands, boyfriends, children, and mother. As they looked at the paintings they remembered their father and they laughed and rejoiced. Their childhoods were becoming present again in the medium of paint. There was a lot of "O Daddy!"—and there was no anger.

May I suggest that you write your will, or if you have one already, reexamine it— as a spiritual exercise? Doing so is a chance to learn humility and objectivity. What

· · · · · ·

we have, we have only for a while. In a will we can let go of our things, including our desire to control others, and possibly create opportunities for God's generosity to be glimpsed through our own willing abandonment. And if we wish to follow the medieval example of Father Wright, we can even let go of our ownership of our soul.

. . . . . .

GLENN PETER was an attractive young man of energy and enthusiasm who, on the 139th day after his twenty-first birthday, died suddenly from a fatal weakness hidden inside his body. No one knew he was sick; no one got to say good-bye. He was, as it were, with us at dinner, and the next morning he was gone.

I had known him for, as it turned out, half his life. When I was a new rector, a priest from a neighboring parish phoned to say he had run into one of "mine" at the hospital. I went to visit, and there was this blond-haired fellow of nine or ten who had just had minor surgery. I spoke with his mother, and they all started to come back to church. Mom, Glenn, and five other siblings: this family alone completely filled a pew.

For many years Glenn was my faithful crucifer. He got confirmed along the way but throughout high school never stopped serving at the altar. Yet he wasn't particularly pious: just serious, and reliable. He was a foreman in his parent's construction company, capable of wielding responsibility over men twice or even three times his age. Having so many fellow-workers, and friends, and siblings with their friends, and parents with a business that touched hundreds, and having died so abruptly and so young, Glenn's was the most massively attended funeral I have ever had.

Our church holds maybe 150 people, and an hour before the service every seat had been taken. Policemen were at the road making people park there and walk up to the church. We crammed people into the offices that are to the side of our nave. People stood in every available square foot of floor. They stood in the narthex, and they stood

. . . . . .

outside, silently (I was later told), catching every now and then a fragment of the words of the service. It was a dark November day, with low clouds blowing quickly over, a day of a strange silence. Four hundred people had come; a thousand more had stayed away.

What is a preacher to say to a church packed with teenagers and twenty-somethings, with workers and students, with so many grieving hearts? What do you say about a life of just twenty-one years and 139 days?

We all were saying that it was too short: that a person is not supposed to die so young. But that way of putting it is not quite right. God did not create us to die; death at *any age* is something that shouldn't be. Death is ever a cheat, a corruption of our humanity, the severing of soul and body that God intended to be united forever.

We were also saying that we grieved the loss of potential: he was so young, there was so much still in his future left for him to do. Yet that, too, is not quite right. Every human life, no matter what its length, falls short of its potential. There are masses of people who look back with melancholy to when they were twenty-one; they think of all the things that, at twenty-one, they imagined they might do, and they realize how few of those things have actually come to pass.

Glenn in his dying showed something that is true of every life: that every one of us is going to be cut short from achieving what we might; and, what is the same thing, that there is something fundamentally wrong with our human condition, something wrong that we experience in death. It's not that all the rest of us at the funeral were okay but there was something wrong with Glenn. There was indeed something wrong with Glenn's physical heart, which suddenly failed him. But the meaning of his life and

. . . . . .

death is not in his heart muscle but rather in what he shows us: there is something wrong with every human heart.

We read in John 11 that Jesus heard his friend Lazarus had died, and when he got close to the home, Martha, Lazarus's sister, came running out to meet him. "Lord," she said, doubtless with tears, "if you had been here, my brother would not have died."

We all wondered, when the news reached us about Glenn, what if we had been there when it happened. The medical evidence is rather strong that there is nothing that any person could have done at that moment. Yet I had a church full of teary people who would have changed places with him, if only they could.

Sometimes very honest words are spoken at the time of death. Such were the words that Lazarus's sister cried to Jesus: "If only you had been here, my brother would not have died." In my sermon, I gave voice to the thought of many when I said, "Jesus, if only you had been in Pawling on Tuesday, Glenn would not have died." Jesus' answer is recorded in John's gospel. *Your brother will rise again.*

To which one might say, "I know—or at least I hope—that I will see him again in heaven."

But heaven isn't the point. Jesus says: "I am the resurrection and the life; he who believes in me, though he die, yet shall he live, and whoever lives and believes in me shall never die. Do you believe this?" Martha answered, "Yes, Lord; I believe that you are the Christ, the Son of God, he who is coming into the world."

So Martha first believes that she will see her brother again in a future beyond the grave. Jesus redirects her hope and says that *he is* that future: *I am the resurrection and the life.* If you believe in Jesus, you will not die forever; eternal life is Jesus himself, and he gives it to us on the Cross. Lazarus has died; Glenn has died; but Jesus has died for all of us, arms stretched out to embrace the world.

The day of Glenn's funeral is indelibly imprinted on the minds of those who knew him. I will never forget it. And I think that for those who were his age, his close friends, his brothers and sisters, there are a lot of days in their life that they will forget, but never that one. The spiritual question is, what does one do with a day such as this? There are two alternatives. One can say, "I have loved someone, and now he is gone," and one can pull back from loving others, and turn in a cynical direction, and say to Jesus, "You weren't there when Glenn needed you; why should I believe?"

Or: one can allow the remembrance to soften the heart, letting the pain of this loss make one more loving, not less; allowing it to fashion in you a person who sees the fragile beauty in every human being. This is to choose faith and not cynicism, and it is the choice I made. I professed in public what I now say in print, that I believe that Glenn did not die alone, that Jesus was there, catching, embracing Glenn on his way to the ground, like a shock absorber, and making Glenn's broken heart his own.

. . . . . .

THERE WAS A FAMINE in the land and the Lord instructed the prophet to go to a certain place where a widow would assist him. *I have commanded her*, the Lord said, *to feed you.* (1 Kings 17:8–16)

But when Elijah got to that designated place, he discovered that the widow had apparently not received the message. He found her gathering sticks near the gate of the city. He told her to go and bring him some water. She started out on that task, when he called her back. "Also bring some bread for me to eat." At this request, she spoke. "Sir," she said, "I have at home only a tiny bit of meal and oil, and even now I was gathering sticks so that I could cook one final bit of bread, that my son and I might eat it, and then die." To which the prophet said, "Make some for me, and then you can make some for your son and yourself." And he promised her that, as long as the famine continued, her jars of meal and oil would not completely run out.

The woman trusted the word she heard from Elijah, and her faith was rewarded with the miracle. She gave away what she had, only to find that God had replenished her stock. As we say in the church on Stewardship Sunday, "You can't out-give God."

But what I want to know is: Why did God fall down on the job? Not the job of keeping food in the larder; that, we have seen, God did very well. No, I mean the job of communication. He clearly told Elijah that he had commanded this widow to take care of him; yet, when Elijah arrived, the widow had apparently heard nothing. She even protests, with the unsurpassable, passionate eloquence of a mother defending her child, that she can't give the prophet that which, the reader knows, God has said he has already commanded her to give him.

We can ask the question another way: When did God speak to the widow? Now the answer appears. God spoke to her when Elijah spoke to her. Elijah had to ask her to do something, in order for her to hear God's call to her to do something.

I hate asking people to do things. For one thing, I'm shy, and for another, as a priest, a lot of the things I ask for have a personal angle. "Sorry to bother you about this, Fred, but the rectory roof is leaking again"—that sort of thing. And again, because I'm their priest, I know a good deal about the pressures in people's lives, and I hardly want to add to them. To complete the list, I don't like conflict. I would much rather describe a situation, and let people come around on their own. At the Cathedral of Saint John the Divine the signs don't tell people what to do. Rather, they read, "Entry here destroys hedge." That's what I'd rather do: just give you information and let you draw your own conclusion.

But Elijah had to ask. The widow would not have experienced the miracle of generosity if Elijah had not asked for what he wanted. God sent Elijah, but Elijah had to ask.

There is, I have decided, a priestly obligation to overcome reticence and ask clearly for what, it would seem, God has already asked. I want my people to make the Eucharist more important in their life than school sports. I want them to support and celebrate the Easter Vigil. I want them to tithe, and to care for the poor, and to have a heart of compassion for the lost. I want them to celebrate children, and to discourage abortion. I want them to stay with the dying and visit the homebound, so that no one is abandoned.

I have to face the absolutely frightening fact that if I don't ask them to do these things, they may never hear God's asking.

· · · · · ·

# The Clerk
. . . . . .

A FEATURE OF MODERN SHOPPING is that one has to deal with people who are strangers. The corner hardware store may be run by someone known to us. But one does not venture into the typical shopping mall seeking familiar human beings with whom one has anything worthy of being called a "relationship." The cashier may smile at us, or scowl; he may say, "Have a nice day"—or say nothing. None of that really matters, because to the harried super-mall cashier you or I am just another anonymous consumer, and to us the cashier is just an appendage to the cash register. Things are structured so as to keep us from being human beings to one another. The typical purchase at the typical place might just as well be conducted by robots.

This I was thinking, until the other day when I was caught short by an unusual event at an otherwise ordinary cash register. It began when the clerk mumbled something, gave a sort of halfway smile, and started ringing up the goods. Each item had a terribly long code number on it, and there seemed to be no scanner (perhaps it was broken). Oh my! We're having to wait an extra thirty seconds while the clerk enters all those code digits. I was watching her do this with, I'm ashamed to say, little patience, when I noticed her hands. Her fingers were curled and rigid; she really had use only of her thumb and forefinger.

Perhaps you know the embarrassed feeling of having not noticed something about another person that you should have. I fumbled some remark about the weather. She smiled again and . . . mumbled. Then, again I'm ashamed to say, I looked at her face for

. . . . . .

the first time. I saw the lines there—lines of stroke, possibly, or muscular disease. Her lines, her hands, her slighted syllables, all together brought a halt to my consumerist impatience. I began to imagine—a determined effort to learn and master a skill against obstacles and a manager who had obviously seen the person within. I doubt I was very good at bridging the inhumanities of the cash register. But I left the store with a renewed hope that humanity, having survived communism, might outlast consumerism too.

*Then they also will answer, "Lord, when did we see thee . . . ?"* (Matthew 25:44)

· · · · · ·

THERE IS A VERY WISE PHRASE in the first sentence of Romans. Paul is writing about "the gospel concerning [God's] Son" and he says he "was descended from David according to the flesh and designated Son of God in power according to the Spirit of holiness by his resurrection from the dead." Here you have in a single sentence Jesus' birth (descended from David) and his death (from which he was resurrected). The key to Christmas is to hold those two ends of life together.

In my parish I run a continual battle to keep Christmas from turning into a child's feast. The problem is that if you try to celebrate Christmas simply from the point of view of a child, you miss what Christmas means. You end up with nostalgia, which is thin gruel. I know my people, so I can speak humorously with them to make a point. Here's what I said to my adults one Advent, right after reading that first sentence from Romans:

> The reality is that we can't, once we pass a certain point, go back and recreate our childhood Christmas. Dear ones, may I speak frankly with you? You aren't as cute as you used to be. There are new kids in town, and all your aunts and uncles are looking at them. You will never again be the center of Christmas the way you once were; never again, with child's eyes, will you peek around the corner into the darkened living room and see the magic tree lights and wonder what is under the tree. You can try. You can go to the mall and sit on Santa's lap, maybe (if you're

· · · · · ·

*able*); but everybody will laugh, because they know you are trying to do what's impossible. George Bernard Shaw, I think it was, said that the problem with youth is that it is wasted on the young. You know what I mean? Then you know the feeling that your own youth was wasted on you, that you had all those wonderful Christmas experiences when you were too young to enjoy them, and now that you understand how wonderful and magical they were, you are too old to have them!

The good news is that once we stop trying to get back to our childhood Christmas, the pleasure of Christmas returns, not from our past but from our future. We adults can understand Christmas if we approach our childhood from the perspective of our death. Only an old man has a chance of understanding a child. If you have wrestled with your own mortality, if you have felt the early twitches of death, if you have come to terms with the fact that in the end you have nothing to take with you but, perhaps, a pinch of holiness, then you can understand a child. Saint Nicholas is always painted as an old man. He has the wisdom of humility, which means the wisdom of the earth, *humus*, dust that O Adam thou art and unto which thou shalt return (as we say on Ash Wednesday). Saint Nicholas, an old man with a pinch of holiness, has the power of resurrection. He can rescue children from slavery, sailors from drowning, a little girl from her dreadful fears; he can give away gold and chocolate and know and be understood by children.

If we try just to enjoy the baby and the presents, if we try to *go back* to the Christmas experience of our past, we can be only ridiculous and pathetic, like some poor aged sot trying unsuccessfully to balance himself upon Santa's knee. We don't fit there anymore. But when we know we are mortal, doomed to die, then we can reapproach our childhood *from the other side*, and rediscover it for the first time. It is the squeezing together that's important, the holding within a single sentence the beginning and the end.

IS IT A CHORE OR A BLESSING? The annual meeting seems chore-like enough, a consequence of the fact that the parish is a religious corporation under the laws of the state. Yet it also has a potential spiritual benefit, if we approach it as an opportunity for discernment.

The burden of making that happen falls mostly on the rector. But fortunately it is a light burden, particularly once one learns the recipe for the annual meeting address. The recipe is not copyrighted, and so I am happy to disclose it. (1) Include at least a short homily. Do not give a mere "state of the parish" talk, but take your people back to the wellsprings of Scripture and theology. (2) Summarize the significant public moments in the life of the parish in the year just past. (3) Encourage your people, and hold out a vision for them.

Let me give an example of how this works. *Homily part:* Last year we had the story from early in Luke's gospel about Jesus teaching from the boat, and afterwards instructing Simon Peter to let down a net. Simon cooperates under protest, since they had not caught a single fish the night before. But he does cooperate, and the net, as we know, becomes so full it nearly tears, and two boats nearly sink under the weight of the catch. Simon realizes that he is in the presence of the God who made both fish and himself, and he hears that Word tell him that his new occupation will be to fish for people. God's Word has been spoken, and God's Word has placed a mission upon those of us who hear it. *Message: we who are here have heard the Word and as a result God has placed upon us a mission.*

*Significant events part:* In the year 2000 our parish paved its long uphill driveway, replaced its broken bell, and installed a sound system—three high-cost and high-profile items that I mentioned. We also continued to give away ten percent of our pledged income to missions, and I was able to read a note of thanks that we received from the sister of Father Marc Nikkel, the missionary to the Sudan who had died during the year. Reviewing the year further brought to mind the number of deaths among us, culminating in the tragic sudden loss of twenty-one-year-old Glenn. His funeral not only brought out a hundred parishioners but also maybe three hundred townspeople who had known him or his family. It fell to me to state that, in God's mysterious economy, that service may have been the most significant spiritual event of our year, since, through the sobriety of death, a crowd of people had been brought quite near to the holy mystery of life. *Message (mostly unspoken): the significant events of our year were done for others.*

*Vision part:* Let me take you around our church. Outside is the churchyard with its graves and columbarium walls. Inside is the font, where life is regenerated in Christ. Between those two places falls much celebration: fairs, potlucks, videos, coffee, private talk, receptions. And in the midst of it all stands the altar, the focal point of every true celebration in this life and the next. Each of us is a pilgrim on our way, from font to altar to grave, to a place we will truly be able to call home. Scripture warns us against attachment to this world. And yet it is a wonderful, dear place, created by God for us; a place that our Lord Jesus desired (over all other possible places) to enter, and dwell within, and love, and redeem. We die; we are born; we celebrate. A parish church is a place where death and birth and celebration are not only put in heavenly context, but rooted in this earth. And for us pilgrims, it is the most wonderful place in the world. *Message (spoken only with the eyes): I am happy to be your rector, and never happier than when you are here with me.*

· · · · · ·

FOR YEARS, whenever my knee acted up, I had joked about "too many genuflections." Then one summer the pain became continuous, and there was a swelling that even I could see, so I overcame my male-denial that I could possibly need a doctor and entered the routine of end-of-the-century medical care in the United States. I first went, as most of us must do, to my primary care physician, who ordered X-rays and sent me to a specialist. Still in male denial, I let a month pass before I saw the specialist who prescribed physical therapy. Another month passed without improvement, then he ordered an MRI. When he saw the results, he sent me to an arthroscopic knee surgeon. Surgery was scheduled for mid-December.

The routine is that a few days before surgery you appear at the hospital for "pre-op testing." I had accompanied my college-age son to pre-op testing the year before, at the same hospital: they had drawn blood and made him sign papers, and that was that. My journey was not so straightforward. When the nurse instructed me to pull up my shirt and lie down, I indicated that although I was no expert in these matters generally in my experience blood was drawn through the arm. She told me that she'd do that later; first I had to have an EKG. "Oh, that's nice," I said, rather incoherently, and obediently allowed her to attach the sticky pads. I tried small talk, then: "You know, a year ago my son had same-day surgery here, and they didn't do an EKG." She smiled at me, gentle young nurse that she was, and (without using the word) indicated that age might have something to do with it.

When I was finished, the nurse gave me a slip and told me to take it down a certain corridor to a certain window. The slip turned out to be an admission ticket to an X-ray room. "Do you have an undershirt on?" the tech asked me.

"Yes," I said, "but they're going to do surgery on my knee."

"We need a chest X-ray," he said.

"But last year, my son—" I began, but didn't try to finish. I already knew the answer.

. . . You start to mull over these things. There was the family photo . . . when was it? Eight years ago? Your father came to visit, your *father*! He looked at it and said: "That's a good picture of your family, son, and of you, a middle-aged man." You were getting a haircut, daydreaming, when you glanced down and saw the collection of hair-clippings in your lap: half-gray. Just yesterday they were deep brown! And now this knee, this pain, this EKG, this X-ray, and (on the day of surgery) this strap on your wrist that says "AGE: 44."

And as the gurney turns into the operating suite, the doors automatically opening, you start to laugh. Years ago someone had told you what Saint Francis called his body, and now *you get it*. With great wisdom, with loving acceptance of the ridiculousness of mortality, Saint Francis called his body "Brother Ass."

. . . . . .

FRED CRADDOCK, the famed preacher and professor of preaching, once told a group of us at the College of Preachers about addressing a gathering of doctors. Rather than throwing around medical jargon or pretending a pseudo-medical expertise, he began with some light joking and then admitted that he had nothing to say to them. Then, with words, he drew a picture of an operating room with all its technological sophistication: the anesthesiologist, the surgeon, nurses, sterilized implements, beeping monitors. He then said that he knew nothing about all of that. His only claim on their attention was that his was the body upon which they were operating. "That person on the table: I'm here to speak to you as him."

A priest often accompanies people to the hospital, but it's one thing to accompany someone, quite another to be the person on the table. I was unprepared for the difference. As a patient in the same-day surgery ward, I first went through what my priestly mind could see was a liturgy of separation such as happens in the preliminaries to baptism. I was taken away alone. I had to strip and put on a hospital gown, placing my belongings (my clothes, my old identity!) in a basket. I got on a bed, and an IV was inserted into my arm, bringing a fluid into my veins that seemed cold and intrusive. My knee was, quite uncomfortably and at tedious length, shaved. Things happened behind me that I couldn't quite see. The surgeon and the anesthesiologist made their visits, asking (I hoped with no irony) if I had any final questions. ("Yes," I wanted to say; "what do you mean by 'final'?") Then other persons arrived, who began to roll the bed, which had become a gurney.

. . . . . .

I was on my way between two worlds. Simply being pushed along in a rolling bed was an unusual experience. I felt my blood move differently, and a kind of dizziness overtook me; I noticed turning corners and yet couldn't see exactly what was happening. Horizontal is not vertical. I sought analogies in amusement park rides, or in driving on ice, but no analogy fit. Nothing in my previous experience was quite like the helplessness, the out-of-control movement that is neither frightening nor calming, of being pushed on a gurney.

I remember the doors opening at my feet, and being able to lift my head enough to see a beautiful view of the Hudson Valley. "This is the doctors' favorite operating room," the nurse told me. Behind me, the voice of the anesthesiologist said I would shortly go under, not to worry, there might be a slight burning sensation.

Baptism is like this: separation, unclothing, moving to a new view, placed entirely in another's hands, the promise of something better to come, and then going under.

The last thing I saw was the crucifix.

# Waking Up

· · · · · ·

THE FIRST THING I saw was the crucifix.

It was directly in my vision. I heard voices, but no one was close by. Turning my head a little, I saw the surgeon and some nurses across the room. One of the nurses came over to me. "Take some deep breaths," she said.

I felt heavy, groggy. Going under anesthesia is like dying; in fact, some of my medical friends have tried to explain to me how anesthesia draws you partway toward death. So to awake from anesthesia is to experience something like resurrection: life given back. But to be told something and to experience it are two different things.

The surgeon, seeing me stir, came to my side and assured me things had gone well. He also began to share details that I realized I couldn't hang on to. Mental triage kicks in at such times: I don't need to understand this now; I'll ask him about it next week. In the meantime I wanted to close my eyes.

Time floated by. A minute? . . . twenty? I wasn't sure. "I see the crucifix," I said to the nurse at my right. Pertly, and with just a touch of dismissal, she replied, "Of course; this is a Catholic hospital. When we opened last June, Sister was up here, and she was very precise about where she wanted the crucifixes. Everything else, she didn't care; but the crucifixes . . ."

I was waking up, and I thought—in a blurred fashion—of how so many of the daily collects depict sleeping and rising as metaphors for death and resurrection. "O God, who art the life of all who live, . . . and the repose of the dead: We thank thee for the timely blessings of the day, and humbly beseech thy merciful protection all the night. Bring us, we pray thee, in safety to the morning hours; through him who died for us and rose again. . . ." That's from daily Evening Prayer. From Morning Prayer: "O Lord, our heavenly Father, almighty and everlasting God, who hast safely brought us to the beginning of this day . . ." And there is a special prayer for use in the evening: "O Lord, support us all the day long, until the shadows lengthen, and the evening comes, and the busy world is hushed, and the fever of life is over, and our work is done. Then in thy mercy, grant us a safe lodging, and a holy rest, and peace at the last."

Somewhere nearby a voice said, "Take some deep breaths." I felt queasy and yet not; dizzy and yet not. I was a traveler in a new land, a person re-crossing a familiar threshold but without, yet, a feeling of familiarity. My eyes kept going back to the crucifix. "You've been here," I thought. "You crossed our threshold. You know what it's like to wake up in a new place. You took on our daily sleeping and rising. You have slept on hard beds. You have taken on excruciating pain. You died and woke again. You've been here."

That, more or less, is what I was thinking. "God the Father gave his Son anesthesia, and he woke up a human being." But today as I write this I realize how important it is to get the verbs right. The incarnation is not a past event but a present one. We look, as we must, through the lens of time. But the figure on the Cross is never a past figure: he is always present. One should say, not only that he slept on stone, but that he *sleeps* on stone today (whenever any person sleeps on sidewalk), and he *feels* the alien IV needle and its chill fluid, and he *experiences* the sleep of anesthesia.

You've been here—no, no, no; you *are* here.

. . . . . .

CHURCH HISTORIANS caution us against transposing our current conceptions of proper church atmosphere back to earlier ages. In the medieval period the church was likely to be the only large building in a village, and a cathedral would be without question the most significant public place in its environs. So if you went to a cathedral, you would be entering a special place of protection from the cold, wind, and rain. You could conduct your business, and you probably would. You could meet neighbors and talk, and you probably would. All this might go on any time, even if somewhere up front a priest was mumbling through the liturgical forms of the mass.

In the great cathedrals, of course, all these elements of human life were cut into the stone, unified within one, great, over-arching synthesis. Think of the little carvings of farmers, crops, masons, smiths, and all the rest, stuck in corners and arches and wherever else they might fit, between the dreams of saints and the nightmares of gargoyles. The point is that both the highest mysteries and everyday human intercourse—everything of significance to human life was conducted within a single edifice which itself proclaimed a glorious vision of redeemed humanity.

In small towns today, churches still make a mark on the skyline. But they are often locked. And in cities, churches are often short, stubby buildings squeezed between buildings torqued high by modern steel and reinforced concrete.

Where then are the modern cathedrals? They are actually all around us, and nearly every county in our nation has one. You'll see them everywhere, once you recollect that ours is a post-Christian society.

The cathedral of my Mid-Hudson Valley, to take one of them, is called the Galleria. When you drive towards it (and of course you must drive there), you will find it on an elevation, rising above the highway, surrounded by a sea of blacktop. It is a white building, particularly striking at night when it is lit up.

Enter the Galleria, and you will find all the elements of a medieval cathedral. There are benches here and there, and, in a large space, the "food court," a gathering court where people sit to exchange information, perhaps make deals. There are vast wide halls along which lovers may stroll, larger groups may shove along, and individual pilgrims make their private way. The central ceiling is vaulted high and down from it streams light both natural and pleasantly artificial. You will find ivy and other green plants throughout. Just off the exact center of it all is an indoor pool with a gracious waterfall. You can sit on the edge of it; many people toss pennies into the pool.

Along the perimeter, of course, are the stores, nearly a hundred of them. In the windows of the stores, and sometimes printed upon temporarily blank walls, you will find the religious images. They are the icons of the vision of humanity that the Galleria proclaims. Real humanity, our cathedral assures us, is humanity that looks like this: gorgeous bodies, wearing *this* underwear, *this* top, *this* outfit, *these* glasses and shoes.

The sacrament of the Galleria is the purchase. But you can enjoy the space without buying anything, just as a medieval peasant could go to the cathedral and not receive Communion. Sip some coffee, see a friend, and be surrounded by the post-Christian icons of our time.

. . . . . .

A FEW YEARS AGO Father Sergei, a Russian Orthodox priest, spent two semesters at General Seminary studying military chaplaincies. Father Wright, of the seminary, thought we'd like each other, and suggested to me that I have him visit my parish and be a guest preacher.

He turned out to be a wonderful house-guest for the weekend. His English was halting, with a fractured syntax and occasionally hilarious mispronunciations. He too would laugh, for he delighted in the play of language. He also liked puzzles and riddles. In fact, he told a riddle to my children that my grandfather, an Oklahoma farmer who never got past the eighth grade, told me when I was a child.

*There was an old man who was going to the bazaar to sell his hat. On the way, three soldiers stop him and ask him what he is doing. He says, "I am going to sell my hat." "How much do you want for it?" they ask him. He answers, "Twenty-five rubles." The soldiers see it is a good hat and they want to buy it, but they have a problem: it is impossible to divide 25 into three parts equally. So they say to the old man, "Here, please take 30 rubles for your hat." The old man took the 30 rubles and sold his hat to the soldiers. But as he walked back towards his home, he thought that it was not right for him to take so much. Seeing a boy nearby, he gave him the extra five rubles and asked him to run back to the three soldiers and give them the money. The boy does so, but when he has explained his errand to the soldiers, they ask each other, "How can we divide five rubles amongst the three of us?" They decided to keep one ruble each, and to give the boy the two rubles for the job he had done. Now we may count up all the money. The soldiers each paid nine*

*rubles for the hat; that makes 27 altogether. They gave the boy two rubles; that makes 29. But the*
*soldiers originally paid 30 rubles. Where is the other ruble?*

That's the Russian version, more or less. Change the hat to a horse, and the rubles to dollars, and you have the version that my Oklahoma grandfather told me decades ago when I was a boy. I felt like the red-dirt peanut fields of Oklahoma had become outskirts of Moscow.

We had announced in the papers that he would be speaking on military chaplaincies during our service, and as a result there were a dozen or so visitors that Sunday who came specifically to hear Father Sergei. During coffee hour afterwards, one of them approached him and spoke sternly. "You need to speak clearer, louder. Learn to project your voice!" Obviously the man didn't realize how little English Father Sergei had at his command, or how he struggled with the correct emphases. The man spoke brashly, and I was embarassed. But Father Sergei just nodded and said, perhaps comprehending, perhaps not: "Thank you." Afterwards when we were alone I apologized for the man's rudeness. But Father Sergei didn't mind. "If he is wrong, it doesn't matter to me. And if he is right, he is my friend for teaching me something." His equanimity amazed me.

Now if I am criticized, I respond defensively: I will withdraw, or attack, or endeavor to prove that the criticism is ungrounded. But Sergei just stood there. "Yes. . . . Thank you."

His quiet humor, his love of children, his way of saying godly truths earnestly had caused many in our parish so quickly to bond with him. We persuaded him to come back for the Triduum, culminating in the Easter Vigil. Our parish celebrates the Vigil in the middle of the night, beginning at 10:30 P.M. and continuing for several hours. Afterwards there is a festive breakfast. At about 2:30 A.M. Father Sergei gave us a toast.

· · · · · ·

We asked him what he thought of our Vigil. "Very good liturgy," he said, and then, pausing, added, "but a little short."

When he got on the train to return to New York City, I thought I would never see him again. But he said that it was possible—one never knows what God may do. As it turned out in God's strange providence, four years later I was part of a theological conversation in Moscow. Our group went on an excursion to the venerable monastery of Sergiev Posad where, indeed, we met Father Sergei. And three years after that he came back to the U.S., this time with his family, as guests of the Presiding Bishop. We may yet meet again in this life. And in the life to come, perhaps he will meet my grandfather and ask him the riddle about the man who sold his hat.

IT'S EASY TO GO THROUGH LIFE without being aware of how we are related to the animals. Recently an animal's life came close to mine for about half an hour, and I'm still thinking about it.

I don't recall who was on the telephone with me. I do recall wondering why the window hadn't broken. The thump was as loud as a rock crash. The evidence stuck to my windowpane: feathers.

"A bird just bounced off my window," I said. "I'll call you back." Outside of my office lay a robin, belly to the ground, wings spread. Was it dead? Only by bending close could I tell there was breathing.

Fearing to harm it, I sat close, watching. The bird was perfectly still. Perhaps, I thought, it would like some water? I got a glass, let a few drops fall on its beak. A sudden shaking followed. Now it was on its legs, standing, its wings pulled into its body. To my relief, it didn't seem to have any broken bones. But it didn't move again.

I poured out a few more drops of water, and it lifted up its beak. A few more, and it opened its beak. I was aiming the drops down its throat, and it was clearly enjoying them. I lowered the glass, and soon the most incredible thing happened—the robin caught the rim of my glass in its beak!

Why do we humans get such a thrill when we brush close to wild creatures? For me, even though the deer around our home are all-too-common animals, sorrowfully overpopulated and crowded out of their woods, still, when I see deer up close, I feel that

· · · · · ·

something like magic has occurred. Coming home from jogging, I have startled them, their white tails bounding into the wood. The story says that Adam named the animals. And Francis, with bird on shoulder, watches over many a courtyard.

"Dear Robin," I said, moved to speech (and glad no one was around to hear)—"You are a crazy bird. You have lost your marbles and now you are drinking my water. You shouldn't let me be this close. You are supposed to be afraid of me. What will you do when the cat comes? The fox?"

The bird was no longer interested in water, but I couldn't leave it. I had given it water and now I was responsible. I moved away and sat down to read my mail.

Was it ten minutes later? Suddenly the robin remembered that it was a robin and I was a man, and in a glorious maneuver, lifted itself instantly, smoothly, high over the drive, gliding to a perfect resting in the upper branches of a sycamore tree. Blessing the robin with a smile, I thought of the pleasure it must give God to see us crazy people drink from his hand then take wing and fly.

. . . . . .